W9-BAO-221

THE CHECKLIST OF CHAMPIONS

HOW TO BECOME THE BEST BY PLAYING AT YOUR BEST EVERY DAY

MIKE LIPKIN

The Checklist of Champions: How to Become the Best By Playing At Your Best Every Day
Marquis Livre

First Edition 2016

Environics/Lipkin Inc.
33 Bloor Street East, Suite 1020
Toronto Ontario
Canada M4W 3H1

ISBN 978-0-9732958-6-3

Design and layout by Heather Pirzas

Printed in Canada

TABLE OF CONTENTS

WARM-UP 1

IT MAY BE THE MOST WONDERFUL FEELING IN THE WORLD 3

YOU'VE SURVIVED THIS FAR. NOW IT'S YOUR TIME TO THRIVE 5

THE RULES FOR THE CHECKLIST OF CHAMPIONS 6

WHO ARE THE CHAMPIONS? 12

THE POWER OF A CHECKLIST IN THE AGE OF "VUCA": "HELP ME THRIVE, NOT JUST SURVIVE" 14

1

IDENTIFY YOURSELF AS A CHAMPION 19

I CAN BE THE BEST IN THE WORLD 27

I HAVE A "UNIQUE VALUE PROPOSITION" THAT I CAN EXPRESS TO OTHERS 41

I AM PASSIONATE ABOUT MY CAUSE 47

I CAN THRIVE UNDER ANY CIRCUMSTANCES 62

MY BEST DAYS ARE ALWAYS AHEAD OF ME 73

2

I DREAM LIKE A CHAMPION 79

I DREAM BIG 85

I SHARE MY DREAM.................................... 90

MY DREAM IS ATTACHED TO A DEADLINE.................. 95

MY DREAM STRETCHES ME TO DO MORE 98

MY DREAM UPLIFTS OTHERS TO ACHIEVE
THEIR DREAM... 102

3

PLAN LIKE A CHAMPION 111

UNDERSTAND YOUR ENVIRONMENT: CONTEXT
IS EVERYTHING 130

BUILD A WINNING MINDSET: BE A "CERTAINIST"........... 143

BUILD THE YIN AND YANG OF YOUR "PERSONAL
BRAND PLAN"... 152

A PLAN IS ONLY AS GOOD AS THE PEOPLE YOU
ENROL IN THE PLAN................................... 161

AS THINGS CHANGE, CHANGE YOUR PLAN.................. 167

4

FEEL LIKE A CHAMPION 171

FIRST, CHAMPIONS WILL BE COURAGEOUS 202

SECOND, CHAMPIONS WILL BE EXCITED 202

THIRD, CHAMPIONS WILL BE ENGAGED 203

FOURTH, CHAMPIONS WILL BE AT EASE 204

FIFTH, CHAMPIONS WILL BE GENEROUS 204

5

"PLAY LIKE A CHAMPION TODAY" 207

TRUE CHAMPIONS ARE AUDACIOUS (AWE-DAY-SHUS) 222

BE RESILIENT - THE STARS ALIGN FOR THOSE WHO FIGHT THE GOOD FIGHT AND STAY THE COURSE 229

BE A CATALYST THROUGH COLLABORATION – MULTIPLY OTHERS' POWER SO THEY CAN MAGNIFY YOURS 235

ACT YOUR ROLE 238

REGENERATE YOURSELF 241

WARM-UP

IT MAY BE THE MOST WONDERFUL FEELING IN THE WORLD

YOU'VE SURVIVED THIS FAR. NOW IT'S YOUR TIME TO THRIVE

THE RULES FOR THE CHECKLIST OF CHAMPIONS

WHO ARE THE CHAMPIONS?

THE POWER OF A CHECKLIST IN THE AGE OF VUCA: "HELP ME THRIVE, NOT JUST SURVIVE"

It may be the most wonderful feeling in the world.

It's the moment we get it. We understand it. We appreciate it. We create it. We solve it. We complete it. We win it. We love it.

It may be a sight, a sound, a smell, a taste, a touch, a phrase, an idea, an action, a person, a performance or a situation.

It's a perfection and connection that may last for a second, an hour, a day, a year, a decade or a lifetime.

It may be what drives us. It also may be what drives us crazy. It's what we need and it's what we want.

The lucky ones get it often. And they do it often. They're designed that way. They easily wow others and others wow them. They're smart. They're optimistic. They're balanced. They're beautiful. They're resourceful. They're charismatic. They're natural champions.

The rest of us have to work very hard to earn those states. Our gifts aren't automatic. Our gratification isn't instant. Our enlightenment doesn't happen with the flick of a switch. We need a manual – a set of instructions that is easy to understand and a pleasure to read.

As a social researcher, I listen to people for a living. I watch them. I talk to them. I learn from them. Every year I connect with over 100,000 people, in person and online. Names, places and details may change but the underlying themes are universal. It's about being human. It's about being appreciated and admired. It's about being valuable to people who are valuable to you.

That's why I wrote this book. Thousands of people mentored me on how to be a champion. Now I'm paying it forward.

YOU'VE SURVIVED THIS FAR. NOW IT'S YOUR TIME TO THRIVE

We're living in a world of mind-boggling complexity. Everything is linked to everything. Everyone is linked to everyone else. Change is exponential. Distinction becomes extinction overnight. Today's hero is tomorrow's zero. Every day is an entire career in miniature.

It can seem as though it's impossible to thrive in this constant storm. It can appear impossible to navigate your way through such chaos. It can look like the odds are always stacked against us. That may even be our past experience.

Yet we've survived. We've come this far. What's more, if you're reading this, you've done a lot more than just survive. You've survived well. You've proven you've got what it takes to stay alive in a scary environment. Congratulations.

I predict with certainty that you'll survive no matter what. You'll find a way or make a way to get by. You have the savvy, the sensitivity and the strength to make it through. But that's not what this book is about.

"The Evolution Manual" is simple: do whatever it takes to survive. Listen to your instincts. Procreate and protect your progeny. Preserve yourself. Stick together. It's all programmed into our DNA. But survival doesn't equal success and it certainly doesn't equal happiness. Success and happiness are conscious pursuits that must be made daily.

This book is about thriving. It's about living life like a champion. It's about realizing joy, freedom and full self-expression. It's about being in your sweet spot, buoyed by a sense of purpose and meaning. It's about creating a future by celebrating one day at a time.

THE RULES FOR THE CHECKLIST OF CHAMPIONS:

Use your beginners mind.

Go slow.

Talk about it.

Life is a game that we all play. Sometimes we know the rules but often we don't. That's why we don't always win our fair share of victories. Playing a game without knowing the rules is like flying blind. We tend to crash into things.

So right up front, I want you to know the rules of this book and play by them. There are only three. I believe that the key to personal power is having fewer rules and living by them.

Use your beginner's mind.
Read everything like you've never seen or heard these insights before – even if you think you have. Be consciously fascinated. Consider the possibilities. Don't automatically agree but don't automatically disagree. Ask yourself the question, "What happens if Lipkin's right?" Let the insights in. Allow them to frolic in your brain. Who knows what magic they can create there?

Go slow.
Give it time. Let the insights breathe. Allow them to percolate. It took me two years to create this work, allow yourself a month

to consume it. Go slow. Involve yourself. Savour the satori – your moments of Zen awakening and ability to see your true nature. Practice the practices I share with you. Read it once. Read it twice. Read it three times over.

Talk about it.

We only know that we know when we can help someone else know. Yet until we can verbalize our thoughts in a way that others can understand, we cannot be sure we understand. What other people hear may not be what we say. Until we master our communication, we may be speaking a language that's foreign to everyone else. So talk about what you read. Share your learning and you'll learn more. Pay it forward and your payout will be even greater.

When you're flying high, you never think you're going to crash. When you crash, you can't believe you'll ever fly again. Without a flight plan, there is no flight.

I have flown as high as I dared to dream. For 23 years, I have made an extraordinary living by talking to people. As a global motivator, I have coached over a million people in 43 countries. I live inside conversations. I have learned how to speak in such a way that others want to speak to me.

Like you, I always have to be on. Every presentation is the beginning of a new stream of possibilities or it's the beginning of the end. Yesterday exists only in our imagination. Today is day one. Most the members of my audiences are seeing me for the first time. Many of them will never see me again. They take away an impression that could last a lifetime. They become passionate promoters or avid detractors. There is no middle ground. Every opinion counts because every opinion could be the one that matters.

I love the spotlight. But its glare is harsh. I have to act happy even when I'm far from it. When your role is to inspire people in difficult circumstances, alibis don't count because they're irrelevant. If people aren't inspired into action, I've failed. End of story.

The question is: who motivates the motivator when the motivator isn't motivated? And the answer is that sometimes there is no one to catch me when I fall. There is no hell like a private hell, especially when you're alone in a dark room in a strange city after a tough gig.

The road can wear you away. Fatigue can mess with your mind. Fear can run rampant when your guard is down. And that's what happened to me in March 2011. Doubt became my default position. I thought about all the ways I was becoming irrelevant, clichéd, unsexy and old. The more I thought about it, the more real my thoughts became. My unconscious mind filled me with worry that my conscious mind amplified.

I sounded hollow and unconvincing to myself when I tried to convince others. I fell into a funk. I lost my mojo. The scary thing is how fast the crash can happen. One week, you're cruising along in top gear. The next week, the wall seems to come out of nowhere. I hit it and I hit it hard. That's why walls are there – to stop things from going further.

So where do you go when you don't know where to go? What do you do when you feel like you've come to the end of the road? You've been there, right? You may think you can see it coming, but it's always a nasty surprise. And it's never like the one before.

If you're a professional, you keep on going. You play the part that you're paid to play. Collapse is not an option. But neither is going it alone. Sometimes we can call on the hero within and sometimes the hero within turns into an idiot. A troubled mind is never a source of great counsel, especially when it's your own.

The irony is that I hit the wall more often than most people. Often, to see how far I can go, I go too far. As a mentor once told me, you only know how tall you are when you get in over your head.

The depression that hit me in March 2011 wasn't my first rodeo. I have been through multiple depressions over the past 30 years. I learn from each one but not enough to prevent me from succumbing to the next. The difference is that my recovery time gets faster as I grow older. It's called resilience.

I reached out to my family doctor, Marla Shapiro. Marla is a medical marvel who has received the Order of Canada for her contribution to family medicine. I think she knows everything and everybody who knows anything. Marla referred me to a remarkable psychologist named Irwin Lieberman.

Irwin is a quiet introvert who is humble in style but bold in his insights. He has a unique ability to calm and excite you at the same time. Over the course of a few weeks, Irwin talked me back from the edge. He helped me make sense of my malaise and reignite my spark.

Irwin has the extraordinary ability to listen to people. He gets people talking. He becomes their co-pilot on their journey. He has the uncanny ability to see things as they see things. Then he refreshes their perspective and enables them to resume their flight.

He introduced me to the concept of a "mental lacuna." That was a gap in my personal judgment. At certain times, I focused on my perceived failures to the exclusion of everything else. The truth is that they weren't failures at all. They were the inevitable steps and missteps of life.

As a motivator, I coach people through exactly the situations that Irwin was coaching me through. The moment I laughed at the thought of being counseled by a psychologist on the exact issues I coach others on, I knew I was going to be okay. God has a sense of humour. I'm glad he gave me one.

There is no machine or drug that can help me like Irwin. There is no algorithm I can plug myself into. The power to connect at a deep, visceral level is essentially human. Machines and drugs can augment it but they cannot automate it.

Monthly meetings with Irwin are now one of the non-negotiable actions in my life. He has become one of the co-pilots who help me follow my personal flight plan for success. The truth is, that on average, any airplane will be off course for 95 percent of its flight. It's consistently coming back to its flight plan by recalibrating its trajectory. There is no flight without a flight plan. It begins long before the plane takes off. It continues at the moment of departure and throughout the journey. It doesn't even end on arrival. That's when all the data points are processed to ensure a superior flight the next time.

Your personal flight plan is the path that keeps you on track. It's the control and discipline that protects us against getting lost or distracted. It is a conscious set of hourly and daily actions required to move in the direction of your dreams.

It's the **Checklist of Champions.**

WHO ARE THE CHAMPIONS?

Champions see themselves as champions. They believe they can succeed and their belief becomes self-fulfilling. They are the ones they've been waiting for. They have their own date with destiny and they do whatever it takes to meet it. Champions don't give in; they dig in.

In my book, there are no ex-champions. Once a champion; always a champion. The fields may change, but the champions always rise to the top. They have a spark that burns forever. They go from *citius, altius, fortius* – faster, higher, stronger - to *anticuus, sapientior, fortior* – older, wiser, stronger.

Champions are people who win. Their results speak for themselves. They are demonstrably superior to their peers. They consistently outperform their competition. Season after season they prove they are best in class.

Champions are inspired by their cause. They are animated by their purpose. Their enthusiasm energizes their actions. Passion is their high-octane fuel and they never run on empty. There's no such thing as an apathetic champion.

Champions are born *and* they are made. They have the gift and they become worthy of their gift. They plan their practice and they practice their plan. They do the right things right and they don't get the wrong things wrong. They dream but they don't daydream. They chase the big stuff and they don't sweat the small stuff.

Champions talk the talk and walk the walk. Their words inspire action. Every hour, every day, every week, every month, every year, champions do what needs to be done. No alibis allowed, no excuses permitted, no easy ways out. Champions become the standard by holding themselves to a higher standard.

It's that simple but it's not easy. Like trains have a track, champions have a **checklist**. It focuses them while it sets them free. It's a way of being and doing at the same time.

I study champions for a living. I live with them. I work with them. I coach them. I brand myself as the *Championator*. My mission is to literally turn people into champions. I help people play at their best so they become the best. **In life 80 percent of success is not just showing up. It's learning to play at your best at what you can be the best at. Read that sentence again: 80 percent of success in life is learning to play at your best at what you can be the best at.**

So I will play at my best at communication and coaching because I can be the best in the world in those disciplines. That's the dream I'm chasing in this book. But I can only catch my dream if you catch yours. So let's go catch our dreams together.

THE POWER OF A CHECKLIST IN THE AGE OF "VUCA": "HELP ME THRIVE, NOT JUST SURVIVE"

In the December 10, 2007 issue of the New Yorker magazine, Atul Gawande shares the modern origin of the checklist:

"On October 30, 1935, at Wright Air Field in Dayton, Ohio, the U.S. Army Air Corps held a flight competition for airplane manufacturers vying to build its next-generation long-range bomber. In early evaluations, the Boeing Corporation's Model 299 had trounced the designs of Martin and Douglas. Boeing's plane

could carry five times as many bombs as the Army had requested; it could fly faster than previous bombers and almost twice as far.

The Boeing Model 299 test plane taxied onto the runway. The plane lifted off smoothly and climbed sharply to three hundred feet. Then it stalled, turned on one wing and crashed in a fiery explosion. Two of the five crew members died, including the pilot.

An investigation revealed that nothing mechanical had gone wrong. The crash had been due to 'pilot error,' the report said. Substantially more complex than previous aircraft, the new plane was deemed, 'too much airplane for one man to fly.'

Still, the Army purchased a few aircraft from Boeing as test planes and some insiders remained convinced that the aircraft was flyable. So a group of test pilots got together and considered what to do. They came up with an ingeniously simple approach: they created a pilot's checklist, with step-by-step checks for takeoff, flight, landing and taxiing.

With the checklist in hand, the pilots went on to fly the Model 299 a total of 1.8 million miles without one accident. The Army ultimately ordered almost thirteen thousand of the aircraft, which it dubbed the B-17. And the Army gained a decisive air advantage in the Second World War."

VUCA stands for *Volatility, Uncertainty, Complexity and Ambiguity*. Everything is changing all the time. In the age of VUCA, all our lives are substantially more complex than a Boeing B-17. Just when you think you have a handle on something, it morphs into something else. Without a tool to guide us through the chaos, it's impossible to guard against **OAF** – *Overwhelm, Anxiety and Fatigue*. That tool is **The Checklist of Champions**.

Just like you, I have a digital diary that reminds me of my daily activities and things to do. But my diary is merely there to ensure I don't miss anything. I can have meetings that are all about nothing. I can have to-do lists that just address the basics. I can spend all my time doing what's necessary and urgent. I can boast, "I'm so busy." I can just let it all the activities sweep me along. At the end of the day, I can be tired and frustrated in equal measure. I can make a lot of movement but not a lot of progress.

The Checklist of Champions, on the other hand, transcends the have-to-do's and the must-get-throughs. It focuses us on the crucial actions that transform the mundane into magic. It's a way of holding ourselves to account so we can count on ourselves. That's how we become consciously competent and purposefully potent.

There is no panacea that works perpetually. You have to improve on a proven process every day. That's the way it works in manufacturing. The "Production Champions" have taken the process to the level of Six Sigma. At many organizations, Six Sigma simply means a measure of quality that strives for near perfection. To achieve Six Sigma, a process must not produce more than 3.4 defects per million opportunities.

As humans, we don't live like that. We don't even aspire to come near that achievement. Throughout this book I will show you that raising your bar to the optimal level can generate optimal functioning. Yes, it takes discipline. But discipline is much easier when you have a process to follow and you can measure the results. A checklist also functions like a parachute or an airbag – it will prevent you from crashing too hard or getting really hurt.

Champions find the hours to find the inspiration. The ticket to mastery is work. It takes sweat of both the literal and figurative kind. It's not always pleasurable, but it always lead to pleasure. Pleasure is the prize for doing the work.

Here's a question for you: what do you believe is the number one struggle that torments people in North America? After researching tens of thousands of people over the past two decades, I've discovered it's procrastination and its aftermath, regret. Putting things off because they seem too difficult is a guaranteed path to pain. **The Checklist of Champions will become your vaccination against procrastination. It will help you do as much as you can as soon as you can.**

The champions make an impact because they do what matters. They work on themselves as much as they work on their job. They have a ritual not just a routine. A ritual is a mindful rhythm that is deeply conscious. It's designed to connect you with your higher self and multiply your power. A routine, on the other hand, is automatic. It's a regular schedule that is applied mostly by habit. A routine alone will help you survive but not thrive. Thriving is the province of ritual.

Perform your own personal haka.

Before every game, The New Zealand rugby team (AKA The All Blacks) publicly perform the *haka*. The haka is an ancient Maori war dance that is acted out ferociously by the players. It's a ritual that declares their intention to decimate their competition before every game. Translated from Maori, it says, "All Blacks, let me become one with the land. This is our land that rumbles. It's my time! It's my moment! This defines us as the All Blacks. It's my time! It's my moment! Our dominance, our supremacy will triumph. And will be properly revered, placed on high. Silver fern! All Blacks!"

While other teams are forced to watch the All Blacks perform their haka, with all its gestures and antics, the All Blacks are psyching themselves up for victory. It's no coincidence that they are the reigning world champions.

We all need our personal haka, AKA **The Checklist of Champions**. As a result of researching champions for over 23 years around the world, I have discovered that they continuously, and consciously, take five actions that enable them to win:

The five actions that enable champions to win:

1. They identify themselves as a champion
2. They dream like a champion
3. They plan like a champion
4. They feel like a champion
5. They act like a champion

These are the actions we'll be exploring in these pages. You may already be a champion, you may be one move away from being a champion or you may have miles to go. It doesn't matter. Champions know it's always day one. Every day it all begins all over again. As the Navy Seals say, "The only easy day was yesterday." So let's go celebrate the struggle.

IDENTIFY YOURSELF AS A CHAMPION

I CAN BE THE BEST IN THE WORLD

I HAVE A “UNIQUE VALUE PROPOSITION” THAT I CAN EXPRESS TO OTHERS

I AM PASSIONATE ABOUT MY CAUSE

I CAN THRIVE UNDER ANY CIRCUMSTANCES

MY BEST DAYS ARE ALWAYS AHEAD OF ME

IDENTIFY YOURSELF AS A CHAMPION

Who do you think you are? What are your defining characteristics? What are the qualities that make you unique? When you look in the mirror, what do you see? How do other people perceive your personality? How are you benchmarking yourself against your environment? Are you growing wiser and stronger as you grow older?

Our identity is the essential way we define ourselves to ourselves. It's the expression of who we believe we are. Our self-belief is the filter through which we process the world. As a global coach, I'm constantly amazed at the power of self-beliefs. Often, the only difference between a champion and and a middle-of-the-packster is their belief about their own capacity. It's not the size of the person in the fight. It's the size of the fight in the person.

We are all magnets. We become the perception we have of ourselves. We attract the things and people that reflect what we already are. Our inner world forms our outer world. As we think, so we become. We are all the writers, directors and producers of our own reality show.

We all have beliefs that limit our growth. Even the champions with whom I work have to work through their self-blocks. The difference is champions are willing to take on their bogeymen. They know success is binary: either it happens or it doesn't. It doesn't happen by degrees. Winners get it all. Losers lick their self-inflicted wounds.

Your most dangerous, scary, daunting experiences have happened to you for one simple reason: to help you discover how powerful you really are so you can venture into the future with courage and confidence. Celebrate your greatness.

Once upon a time, there was a young princess who had just completed her martial arts studies under a world-renowned teacher. Her reward for successfully completing her studies was the gift of five weapons from the school. Henceforth, she would be known as Princess Five-Weapons. Armed with her newly acquired knowledge and weapons, she set out on the road leading to the city of her father, the king. On the way, she came to a village at the entrance to a large forest. The people of the village warned her not to enter the forest. They pleaded with the princess,

> "Princess, do not enter the forest. An ogre named Sticky Hair lives there. He kills every person he sees."

But the princess was confident and fearless as a lioness. She entered the forest. When she reached the heart of the forest, the ogre showed himself. He was as tall as a palm tree. His head was as big as a house. He had the beak of a hawk. His eyes were black and bloodshot. His hair was as long and slithery as a thousand pythons. His belly was covered with blotches. His hands and feet were dark green. He gave off a rotting stench.

"Where are you going?" the ogre demanded.

"Halt!" shouted Princess Five-Weapons with great confidence,

> "You are my prey, Ogre, be careful about attacking me. I have arrows steeped in poison. I will kill you where you stand."

Having thus threatened the ogre, the young princess put an arrow to her bow and let fly. The arrow stuck to the ogre's hair. The princess shot another twenty arrows at the ogre. All stuck to the ogre's hair. The ogre shook his head and all the arrows fell to the ground. He advanced towards the princess. But the princess was not afraid. She threatened the ogre a second time and, drawing her sword, she delivered a masterly blow. Once again, the sword stuck to the ogre's hair. Then the princess smote the ogre with a spear. That also stuck to the ogre's hair. Then she smote him with a club. That also stuck right to his hair. Then she struck him with her hatchet. It too stuck to the ogre's hair. When the princess saw that all her weapons had stuck to the ogre's hair, she shouted,

> "Master Ogre, you have never heard of me before. I am Princess Five-Weapons. When I entered this forest infested by you, I did not rely on my weapons to slay you. I relied only on myself. Now I am going to beat you and pound you into powder and dust."

Having thus made known her intention, she struck the ogre with her right fist. It stuck to the ogre's hair. She struck the ogre with her left fist. That also stuck. She kicked the ogre with her right foot. It stuck to the ogre's hair. She kicked the ogre with her left foot. That also stuck to the ogre's hair. Then Princess Five-Weapons said to the ogre,

> "I will beat you with my head and pound you into powder and dust."

She beat the ogre with her head. That also stuck right to the ogre's hair. Princess Five-Weapons, stuck five times in the ogre's hair, dangled from the ogre's body. But for all that she was unafraid. She was undaunted. As for the ogre, he thought:

> "This is some lioness of a woman, some woman of noble birth. No mere woman. For although she has been caught by an ogre like me, she appears neither to tremble nor to quake. Of all the humans I have met and eaten, I have never, never known a woman like this one. Why is this woman not afraid?"

Not daring to eat the woman, he asked,

> "Youth, why are you not afraid? Why are you not terrified of death?"

> "Ogre, why should I be afraid?" she replied, "For in one life, one death is absolutely certain. What's more, I have in my belly a thunderbolt for a weapon. If you eat me, you will not be able to digest that weapon. It will tear your insides to tatters and fragments. It will kill you. If you eat me, we'll both perish. That's why I am not afraid."

> "What this youth says is surely true," thought the ogre, terrified by the thought of death. "From the body of this lioness of a woman, my body would not be able to digest even a fragment of flesh as small as a kidney bean. I'll let her go."

And he let the princess go. The princess then admonished the ogre. She warned him never again to eat humans. She transformed him into a spirit entitled to receive offerings in the forest. Then she went back to the village, told the people that the ogre no longer presented a threat and went on her way.

I love this tale because it embraces the universal conflict between fear and courage, life and death, the known and the unknown, trusting yourself versus going with the crowd.

The princess in the story could only prevail because of the "Thunderbolt" she knew she possessed within her. This thunderbolt transcended her five senses. Her five senses were of no use against the ogre. All the training and skills she had acquired couldn't prepare her for the unknown danger of the ogre. It was the princess's innate confidence and courage that empowered her to outmanoeuvre the ogre. When all her external resources failed her, the princess went within. She never hesitated. At no point did she ever doubt that she would not only survive, but that she would subdue the ogre.

There is another reason why I love this story. Often, we only realize and use our power in the most extreme circumstances. Every day, we read about deeds of heroism performed by people who were pushed to the very edge. Until that fateful moment when they were forced to fly or die, these people may have let their power lie dormant within them. It took a colossal, life or death event for them to manifest their power.

Think about your own life. How many times have you been placed in extreme circumstances? Have you noticed that in hindsight everything seems to make sense? The difference between the heroes and the cowards is heroes know that ultimately the right outcome will occur. Cowards get caught in the terror of their worst fears. Bereft of faith, they die a thousand deaths. The hero dies but one.

So release your thunderbolt. Don't wait for your circumstances to become extreme. Declare your identity. Start now. As Oliver

Wendell Holmes said, "What lies behind us and what lies before us are tiny matters compared to what lies within us."

Becoming a champion begins with identifying yourself as a champion. You cannot be what you do not believe. Check out the **Champion Identity Checklist**. Work through it before you move on. Write down your spontaneous responses to the statements. You may be surprised by what you see.

YOUR CHAMPION IDENTITY CHECKLIST:

		Yes	No
1.	I can be the best in the world	☐	☐
2.	I have a unique value proposition that I can clearly express to others	☐	☐
3.	I am passionate about my cause	☐	☐
4.	I can thrive under any circumstances	☐	☐
5.	My best days are always ahead of me	☐	☐

I CAN BE THE BEST IN THE WORLD

In sports, there are certain competitions that require an athlete to meet a qualifying standard in order to participate. That means to compete, they have to hit the mark or surpass it.

For most elite competitions like the Olympics and Athletics World Championships in Athletics, the world governing body publishes standards in advance of the competitions. Entries for these high-level competitions must be selected and submitted by the national governing body. Only two to three athletes per country can be selected for each event.

If you're selected to compete at the event, you know you're literally among the best in the world. You've qualified to perform at the highest level against the best of the best.

Life is like an elite competition. Before you can compete, you have to qualify for it. Only then can you actually win. So my question to you is: have you met or surpassed the qualifying standard? How do you know?

I'll make it easy for you: if you're working for a profitable company that is more than ten years old, you're either meeting or close to meeting the qualifying standard. Anything less would disqualify your company from the competition. Seriously, according to the U.S. Bureau of Labor Statistics: about half of all new establishments survive five years or more and about one-third survive 10 years or more. As you would expect, the probability of survival increases with a firm's age. Survival rates have changed little over time. (source: Washington Post, January 27, 2014) And even if your company has not yet stood the test of time, at least you're in the contest. You've made it to the track. Let's begin from there.

I know I'm among the best in the world every time I make it to the short list of speakers for a major event or coaching assignment. My clients have access to the best talent on the planet. Every competitor on their list is capable of earning a standing ovation. I need to be on a short list at least 300 times a year. That means I need about six enquiries a week (including holidays) to know that I am among the best in the world.

If I fall short of that objective, I know I'm not among the best motivational speakers in the world. I can apply a range of other criteria such as my personal opinions and other people's subjective points of view. But the only criterion that really matters is how often I'm considered for the role.

Every talk that I deliver is a deposit on the next one. My success is a function of both frequency and consistency. In the new transparency, failure goes viral in the click of a button. But triumph travels just as quickly.

I love to win, but I'm thrilled to compete at the highest level. Life is a numbers game. The more times I pitch, the more times I succeed. A "No" is an indispensable step towards "Yes." On average, I need two 'No's" to make a "Yes."

Amateurs sit and wait for inspiration; professionals just get up and go to work. I'm a professional. I am always on when I need to be. There are no off days, just days that require greater effort. Consistency is the hallmark of champions. Like Tim Hortons, we all need to be "Always Fresh."

What's your one real criterion that proves you're among the best in the world? How close or far away are you from achieving it? Who would you need to be in order to be among the best in the world? How would you need to define yourself? Because if you don't define yourself, others will.

Being among the best in the world ensures your survival. There's always a need for someone who consistently delivers world-class performance. But champions have a visceral need to be the best of the best. That means it's embedded in their DNA. It's not just that they have something to prove to others. They have something to prove to themselves. It's not the pursuit of happiness. It's the happiness of the pursuit.

To a champion, fulfilment is *knowing* you're an exemplar: you're a model of what is possible. You represent the highest level of your craft. *Knowing* it to be true goes beyond just *believing* it to be true. When you know it to be true, it becomes who you are, not just what you do. It's a level of confidence that multiplies your motivation to self-actualize your power.

I *can* be the best in the world becomes I *must* be the best in the world. I *must* be the best in the world becomes I *will* be the best in the world. I *will* be the best in the world becomes I *am* the best in the world. Then the cycle begins all over again.

I can be the best in the world is not a boast. It's a declaration. It's a personal line in the sand that propels you forward. Everyone comes into this world as a miracle. And miracles are not designed to be mediocre. Life is about living out all our potential, not passing with it unspent.

This may be a wake up call or it may be a validation of your commitment to personal greatness. It may also appear grandiose. I can almost hear you thinking, "Best in the world !?" But if not you, then who? And if not right now, then when?

If you're working in the United States or Canada, you're working in one of the most competitive, advanced, mature markets on earth. If you can be the best at what you do in your neighbourhood, you may just be the best at what you can do in the world. That was certainly the case for me.

I know I can be the best in the world at motivational speaking and personal coaching. I have proven it. For 23 years, I have delivered 100 talks a year or more. I have been rated the best by the best audiences in the world against the best speakers in the world. I'm not telling you this to impress you. I'm telling you this to impress upon you the necessity of knowing versus just believing.

One hundred is my magical number. If I deliver 100 programs a year and I achieve an average rating of 9/10 or higher, I know I can be the best in the world. I also know that it's dynamic. Every day is my entire career in miniature. Today's blow-away performance can be tomorrow's blowout. But I also know that as long as I chase 100 and an over 9/10 rating, I can be the best in the world. And that's a sweet piece of knowledge to have. It's my turbo-boost when I need it most.

It may not always be possible to make a living at what you can be the best in the world at. You may be an Olympic calibre curler who manages a store. Or you may be a hilarious stand up comedian who sells life insurance. That's okay. In pursuing "best in the world" status in one part of your life, you'll enhance the other. By aspiring to be the best motivational speaker in the world, I become a world-class spouse, friend and colleague. Excellence cascades all around us.

If you want to be the best you can be, create an image of what that "best" looks like. Maybe you need to create your own image or maybe there is an icon you can follow and build on. It may be either someone you know or someone you've studied. Ask yourself: what do they do that makes them great at it? And how can you take it to another level? What does it mean to you to do it? What does it look like and sound like?

Here are some of the exemplars that inspire me to be the best in the world at what I do. Some of them are global icons and some are my local heroes:

Clint Eastwood

Deep into his 80s, he continues to produce extraordinary movies. "I never let the old man in," he says. From being Dirty Harry at 41 to making The Jersey Boys at 84, he continues to delight and astonish the world. My favourite Eastwood quote is, "I tried being reasonable. I didn't like it."

Nelson Mandela

I met Nelson Mandela when he was 84 years old. His eyes sparkled with curiosity and interest. His smile was so warm it made me want to cry. My great insight from him was, "If you want to make peace with your enemy, you have to work with your enemy. Then he becomes your partner."

Michael Adams

Michael is my business partner and founder of the Environics Research Group. He is 70 years old. He has authored six books and been awarded an honourary doctorate by Ryerson University in Toronto for his contribution to social research. Despite his age, he has the enthusiasm and energy of an adolescent. Michael is a bon vivant who has the extraordinary ability to marshal people behind a cause. He has taught me about the strength of "weak ties" – the potential of people on the perimeters of your social network to find you opportunities – and the impact of "soft power" – the ability to attract and co-opt, rather than force and compel. In many ways, I consider Michael the quintessential Canadian.

Kim Yost

The 61-year-old CEO of Art Van, a billion-dollar furniture store chain, headquartered near Detroit, Michigan, Kim is also the ex-head of The Brick, a leading Canadian furniture store chain. Kim is living proof that the more you do the more you learn to do. He is a man in perpetual motion who is constantly generating amazing ideas and executing them with his team. My favourite quote from Kim is, "Don't dig a hole with your mouth, build a springboard through your language."

Dani Reiss

Dani is the CEO of Canada Goose, the manufacturer of goose-down parkas designed to withstand temperatures of -50°C. He continually stuns me with his insights around building both a great brand and a great company. Dani has built the brand around one core attribute, "Made in Canada." As he puts it, "We represent the people of the north. Our brand was built on the backs of the people who live in the coldest parts of the world. We are The Uniform of The North. That authenticity drives people to our brand. Our authenticity makes us fashionable. We're fashionable because we're functional. We're fashion because we're not fashion. If we tried to be fashion, we would not be fashion."

Fauja Singh

Also known as the Turbaned Tornado, Singh is 105 and is believed to be the world's oldest runner. Since taking up running at the age of 89, he has run nine full marathons. On October 16, 2011, Singh completed the Toronto Waterfront Marathon in eight hours, 11 minutes and became the first 100 year old to finish a marathon. "Being active is like a medication," he says, "I don't want to withdraw from that medication." Although Singh may have singular genes, he is evidence of the healthful longevity that can be achieved through good fortune, good training and good lifestyle.

Allison Rosenthal

Allison is the general manager of a leading Japanese pharmaceutical manufacturer based in Montreal, Canada. She is a 40-something mother of two who has the remarkable capacity to simultaneously charm, invigorate and coach the people around her. Allison is on my list of exemplars because she is one of those people who make every meeting with her an experience to be savoured. She loves to talk; she loves to listen and others love to do both with her.

Jim Cramer

Jim is the host of a daily CNBC show on how to invest in the stock market. He is loud and opinionated. But he is also knowledgeable and funny. At 70 years old, he brings the heat to every show, irrespective of his physical condition. I've seen him on air when he can barely speak but he never backs down. He says, "We are all wrong so often that it amazes me that we can have any conviction at all over the direction of things to come. But we must continue to have it." I have personally benefited greatly from Cramer's insights. His daily rants are both entertaining and lucrative.

Jeff Immelt

Jeff is the CEO of General Electric. I have shared the stage with Jeff at a number of GE functions. He can work a room like no one I've ever seen. He can defend GE's acquisition of Alstom, a major French power, transportation and energy company, to the French cabinet and engage an intern with equal skill. He demonstrates an unbridled, boyish enthusiasm for his business and he describes the most complex transactions in a way everyone can understand. He is in constant conversations with core stakeholders and he's damn good at it.

Here's how he claims to spend his time: "You can't delegate growth or customer satisfaction. I'm spending four or five days a month with customers. Twice every month, I do town-hall meetings with several hundred customers to share ideas on GE's direction and listen to their thoughts on what we can do better. And we're doing what I call dreaming sessions with key customer groups, trying to think about where our business and their business will be in five or 10 years. I'm probably spending 30 percent of the time on people, teaching and coaching."

Pope Francis

I'm am not Catholic but Pope Francis alone would make me want to consider becoming one. At the age of 78, he is attempting to make the Church more open, inclusive and accountable. As the Financial Times reported on December 27, 2014, "He scolded members of the Vatican bureaucracy in a harshly worded Christmas greeting that listed '15 ills' weakening their mission – from narcissism to hypocrisy and even 'spiritual Alzheimer's.' Pope Francis is giving his two millennia-old institution the biggest shake up since the Second Vatican Council convened by John XXIII in 1962-65."

Pope Francis's wisdom is encapsulated in two of my favourite quotes:

"Look at the peacock: it's beautiful if you look at it from the front. But if you look at it from behind, you discover the truth... Whoever gives in to self-absorbed vanity has huge misery hiding inside them."

"An evangelizer must never look like someone who has just come back from a funeral."

Stephen King

At the age of 67, King has written 66 books and sold over 350 million copies. As he ages, he is accelerating his output. In 2014 alone, he published two novels – Mr. Mercedes and Revival. King's formula for learning to write well is, "Read and write four to six hours a day. If you cannot find the time for that, you can't expect to become a good writer."

He sets out each day with a quota of 2000 words and will not stop writing until it's met. He also has a simple definition for talent in writing: "If you wrote something for which someone sent you a check, if you cashed the check and it didn't bounce and if you then paid the light bill with the money, I consider you talented."

Here are three other truths from King that will help you become an exemplar:

- "The scariest moment is always just before you start."
- "Monsters are real and ghosts are real too. They live inside us and sometimes, they win."
- "I write to find out what I think."

Tony Bennett and Lady Gaga

In September 2014, Tony Bennett, 89 and Lady Gaga launched their collaborative album, Cheek to Cheek. It was an audacious mash up between artists from two completely different eras. Cheek to Cheek consists of jazz standards by popular jazz composers, such as George Gershwin, Cole Porter, Jerome Kern and Irving Berlin. The album was inspired by Bennett and Gaga's desire to introduce the universal appeal of the songs to a younger generation.

It was an immediate smash hit. Debuting at #1 on the US Billboard 200, it sold 131,000 albums in its first week. Bennett also extended his record as the oldest person to achieve a number-one album on the chart. So what's age got to do with it? Everything and nothing. It's taken Bennett almost 90 years to make everything old new again.

Frank Gehry

At 85, Frank Gehry is unquestionably the leading architect in the world. The new Louis Vuitton Foundation museum in Paris is being hailed by its billionaire patron, Bernard Arnault, as a "masterpiece." And yet, says Gehry, "I'm so insecure. I call it a healthy insecurity; it keeps me going. For me, every day is a new thing. I approach each project with a new insecurity, almost like the first project I ever did. And I get the sweats. I go in and start working. I promised a lot of people I'd slow down when I turned 80. The fact is I'm an opportunist. I would like to make a building as intellectually driven as it is sculptural. I can't just decide myself what's being built. Someone decides what they want, then I work for them."

Gehry's success helped elevate architecture to a prominent place in the culture. Beginning in the late 90s, many institutions started chasing after Gehry-like museums hoping to replicate "the Bilbao effect" and transform their cities. The museum in Bilbao, Spain, designed for the Guggenheim Foundation, was the first building that showed the true creative potential of digital design. The building was also sacrilegious in its approach to art galleries: Its split-level layout included nine galleries of irregular shapes and proportions.

The 1997 opening of the Guggenheim Museum in Bilbao shows how an imaginatively designed museum commissioned by an energetic mayor can help turn a city around. In the first three years after the museum opened, visitors' spending in Bilbao raised over €100m ($110m) in taxes for the regional government, enough to more than recoup the construction costs. In 2012, more than a million people visited the museum, at least half of them from abroad. Other cities without historic cultural centres now look to Bilbao as a model for what vision and imagination can achieve.

Every day your personal community depends on you to be the best in the world. We become a version of the people with whom we work and live. Either we inspire the people around us to be more or we give them permission to be less. We stretch them or we allow them to slack off. The difference between a stretcher and a slacker is the presence of other stretchers or slackers.

Welcome to the world of Wabi-Sabi. Imperfect may be the new perfect.

I was introduced to the concept of **"wabi-sabi"** by Irwin Lieberman in our discussions around ageing, failing, flailing, struggling and living with imperfection. Being the best doesn't mean being perfect. In fact, it's the wear and tear that makes something especially desirable.

Pared down to its barest essence, wabi-sabi is the Japanese art of finding beauty in imperfection and accepting the natural cycle of birth, growth and aging. It's simple, slow and uncluttered. It reveres authenticity above all.

In her book, The Wabi-Sabi House: The Japanese Art of Imperfect Beauty, Robyn Griggs Lawrence writes that wabi-sabi is street markets, aged wood, worn leather, cracked stone. It celebrates creases and crevices and all the other marks that time, weather and loving use leave behind. Through wabi-sabi, we learn to embrace wrinkles, rust, frayed edges and the march of time they represent.

Wabi-sabi is underplayed and modest, the kind of quiet, undeclared beauty that waits patiently to be discovered. It's a richly mellow beauty that's striking but not obvious, one that you can imagine having around you for a long, long time. It's Helen Mirren versus Marilyn Monroe.

For the Japanese, it's the difference between *kirei*, merely "pretty," and *omoshiroi*, the interestingness that kicks something into the realm of beautiful. (Omoshiroi literally means, "white faced," but its meanings range from fascinating to fantastic.) It's the peace found in a moss garden, the mountains meeting the stormy surf, the floral warmth of a superb sake.

Wabi stems from the root "wa," which refers to harmony, peace, tranquility and balance. Generally speaking, wabi had the original meaning of "sad, desolate and lonely," but poetically it has come to mean simple, unmaterialistic, humble-by-choice and in tune with nature. Someone who is perfectly herself and never craves to be anything else would be described as "wabi."

Sabi by itself means "the bloom of time." It connotes natural progression-tarnish, hoariness, rust – the extinguished gloss of that which once sparkled. It's the understanding that beauty is fleeting. It means taking pleasure in things that are old and faded. A proverb emerged: "Time is kind to things, but unkind to man."

Sabi things carry the burden of their years with dignity and grace: the chilly mottled surface of an oxidized silver bowl, the yielding gray of weathered wood, the polished cobblestones of ancient streets. There's poetry in things that carry this patina. We seek sabi in antiques and even try to manufacture it in distressed furnishings. True sabi cannot be acquired, however. It is a gift of time.

So now we have wabi, which is humble and simple and sabi, which is rusty and weathered. Wabi-sabi inspires a minimalism that celebrates the human rather than the machine. They are the items you both admire and love to use, like those hand-crank eggbeaters that still work just fine. Things that resonate with the spirit of their makers' hands and hearts: the chair your grandfather made, your 6 year old's lumpy pottery, a sweater you knitted (out of handspun sheep's wool, perhaps). Pieces of your own history: sepia-toned ancestral photos, baby shoes, worn Converse All Star sneakers, 1960s wind up watches, frayed handbags and briefcases, 40-year-old Parker Fountain Pens, Oxford handmade shoes.

A solid yellow line separates tattered and shabby, dust and dirt from something worthy of veneration. Wabi-sabi is never messy or slovenly. Worn things only take on their magic in settings where it's clear they don't harbour bugs or grime. You sense they've survived to bear the marks of time precisely because they've been so well cared for throughout the years.

If you want to take care of others, take great care of yourself first. It's your flaws that make you perfect.

I HAVE A "UNIQUE VALUE PROPOSITION" THAT I CAN EXPRESS TO OTHERS

No matter what business you're in, you're in the same business as me: meaningful differentiation. That means setting yourself apart from the pack in a way that makes you special and appealing to your audience. It's creating an aura of desire that draws others towards you.

A "unique value proposition" is your distinctive promise that makes you irresistible to others. It's the pull that compels them to prefer you over anyone else. It's how you can solve your customers' problems or find them opportunities in ways that are better than the competition. It's a demonstrably superior contribution to their success.

Sometimes your unique value proposition may not be related to the product itself. It may be related to how you deliver it, how you make it easier or how you make it safer. It depends on your colleagues' or customers' points of view about what's most important.

Your unique value proposition is a kind of magic that transforms the quality of others' lives. It enables them to do what otherwise would have been impossible. Every day, we embrace other's unique value propositions as part of our minute-by-minute lifestyle.

So I'm typing these words on an Apple Macbook Pro. Its unique value proposition is simplicity and beauty in equal measure. I can do things on a Mac that I cannot do on any other technology.

I'm drinking a French Roast Clover-made coffee from Starbucks. Its unique value proposition is consistently, unmatchably delicious coffee personalized to my taste.

I'm wearing my Fitbit exercise tracker wrist-strap. Its unique value proposition is thrilling one-of-a-kind technology that enables me to track my physical activity, heart rate and performance versus my friends.

I'm doodling my thoughts on a writing pad with my Bic Crystal 1.6mm ballpoint. It has a satisfying silky smooth ink flow though a broad nib that costs 23 cents a pen.

I'm sitting in silence despite the noise around me with my Bose Acoustic Noise Cancelling Headphones over my ears. Their unique value proposition: perfect fit and functionality. I can go anywhere and be assured of peace and quiet.

Today, I will manage my customer relationships through Salesforce.com who claim, "We help make your customers love you. Our applications are designed to get new customers, keep the ones you've got and help your team deliver great personal experiences." Who can resist that promise?

Later tonight, I will watch Liev Schreiber as the dark hero in the TV series, Ray Donovan. His unique value proposition is being tough, vulnerable and stylish in a way that allows me to vicariously experience his agony and mastery at the same time.

Tomorrow, I will trade stocks online through TD Waterhouse

Direct Brokerage. Their unique value proposition is empowering me to buy and sell stocks with ease and insight. I have access to quality data and impeccable service provided by my personal account manager, Stephanie Mahoney.

This week, I will book a speaking engagement through the Speakers Spotlight Speakers Bureau. Their unique value proposition is that through the quality of their people and relationships with blue chip clients across Canada, they win me more business than anyone else.

This winter, I will wear my Canada Goose parka on the sub-zero days, freeing me from the cold to do whatever I want, irrespective of the elements.

Think about the brands and people that you choose every day. With hundreds of options available to you, what are the special qualities that have made them indispensable to you? What are your special qualities that make you indispensable to others? In a sentence or less, how would you express your unique value proposition?

Our ultimate value proposition is to become someone who fully represents what others want.

If we know what others like, we can become what they like because we can become like them. Read that sentence again. It's the essence of influence. I guarantee that you and I are alike. We both love inspirational literature and we both love inspiring others. We're enthusiastic and energetic in equal measure. We believe in the promises of life. I am like you and you are like me. That's why you like this book so far.

No one ever says to someone else, "I like you because we've got big differences." Instead we're attracted to people we believe are just like us. The moment someone sees us as similar a relationship begins to evolve. On the other hand, the moment someone sees us as alien the relationship breaks down.

The secret is to like others, irrespective of who they are. If we always look for what we like in others, we're far more likely to see it. What's more, our focus will probably be reciprocated. We tend to like people who show us they like us. Admiration and affection are powerful attractors. But don't just take my word for it. The next time you meet someone new show your interest in them. Express your curiosity for what they do. Demonstrate your regard for their achievements. Declare your fascination with them. And watch what happens…

We understand what people like by understanding the emotions that affect their decisions. We have to align with their deepest animating spirit. We have to mean something powerful to them. If we can arouse their desired emotions, we can move them in the direction we want them to go because it's the direction they want to go.

The most valuable people are those who channel our desires and accelerate their fulfilment. Once again, that's why you're reading this. It's channeling your desires and giving you ways to accelerate their fulfilment.

The emotions that affect my decisions are excitement, eagerness, admiration, mastery, ambition, motivation, connection and inspiring others' success. For anyone to influence me, they would have to show a similar commitment to those emotions and desires.

It's the same with brands. People respond to brands the way they respond to people who make them feel the same way. It's their emotional association with the brand that makes it meaningful. So in addition to the brands I have already mentioned, I love The Ritz

Carlton, Levi's, Ray-Ban, IWC, Gatorade, Audible.com, The New York Times, Moleskin, Blundstone, Canali, Oral B, Under Armour and The Springbok Rugby Team. All these brands epitomize the emotions that make me happy.

It amazes me how few people can express their unique value proposition. Even the most successful people have difficulty articulating it. And it's not because it's so hard. It isn't. They simply haven't worked on it. Somehow, it's not considered right to promote yourself as a one-of-a-kind resource with an unashamedly killer promise.

Let me ask you this question: how often have you almost won an account or a customer or a deal, only to lose it at the final moment? Often, right? You do everything right. The signals are all flashing green. You're on the verge of celebrating. And then you hear that you're not the one or that the customer has changed their mind and gone in a different direction.

Welcome to the tiebreaker marketplace.

A tiebreaker is a special game to choose a winner from competitors who have tied. The players or teams are so similar in quality and performance that something extra is required to decide the winner. In tennis, it's the extra game when the score is six games all. In soccer, it's the penalty shootout. In baseball, it's the 14th, 15th or 16th innings. What's it for you?

In my case, it comes down to this simple question: why should we choose you? Sometimes, it's an explicit question. And sometimes, it's the implied expectation. I know that my ultimate success is a function of how powerfully I can answer it.

So my unique value proposition is:

I give people the proprietary insights to play at their best so they become champions.

That's it. That's my mission. That's what I live for. That's what I chase. That's my commitment to you. I am the *Championator*. Yup, I'm even creating my own vocabulary. Hey, if Arnold can do it, so can I. And so can you.

My unique value proposition is a vital part of my sales pitch. It's a five-second tiebreaker that I deliver with passion and verve. How I say it is as important as what I'm saying. It also enables me to probe what being a champion means in the world of the prospect. I become the conduit to their people's success.

So take a crack at your unique value proposition right now. Tell me why you should win the tiebreaker. Give me a powerful reason to choose you and tell my stakeholders why I chose you. Make it easy for me to justify selecting you against fierce competition. Email me now: **mike.lipkin@environics.ca**

Have some fun. Make some noise. There is nothing like a little humour to make your promise even more serious.

Be a Talisman.

Your happiness is not just your happiness; it determines the happiness of everyone you encounter. I am literally a motivational speaker. But so are you. If you motivate others when you speak to them, you're a motivational speaker. If not, they will vote with their legs and walk away from you.

Happiness can be stored and accessed at will. It can be as simple as a fresh orange or a firm banana. It can be a warm jacket in the winter or comfortable shoes on a long walk. It can be a good friend or a trusted colleague. We've all stored good feelings in things and people around us. They're talismans.

A talisman is anything or anyone whose presence exercises a powerful influence on others' emotions. So in all our interactions with others, we want to be "tagged" as a magical presence in their lives. We need to make every meeting an extraordinary experience because every meeting trains others how to expect us to be in the next meeting. You know that you've become a talisman when the people you want to be with, want to be with you.

My friend and colleague, Ted Langschmidt, tells the story of a child who stole eye-glasses from the orphanage where he lived. He kept them in a box in a hiding place behind the building. When he was caught and asked why he stole them, he confessed that he associated eye-glasses with clever people. By having his own box of "cleverness," he hoped to acquire some of its wisdom. Instead of eye-glasses, I go directly to the source and collect clever people around me. Clever people make me happy.

So *what* makes you happy? *Who* makes you happy? How can you design your world so your talismans surround you?

I AM PASSIONATE ABOUT MY CAUSE

At his 1964 trial by the South African Apartheid Government for alleged sabotage, Nelson Mandela chose, instead of testifying, to make a speech from the dock and proceeded to hold the court spellbound for more than four hours. His speech, which was made at the beginning of the defence case, ended with the words:

> "During my lifetime I have dedicated myself to this struggle of the African people. I have fought against white domination and I have fought against black domination. I have cherished the ideal of a democratic and free society in which all persons live together in harmony and with equal opportunities. It is an ideal, which I hope to live for and to achieve. But if needs be, it is an ideal for which I am prepared to die."

Mandela epitomized the spirit of a champion. According to the Oxford Dictionary, a champion is someone who vigorously supports or defends a cause. It's when you're willing to put someone or something ahead of yourself. It means putting yourself at risk because you believe in the magnitude or merit of something else.

When you're passionate about your cause, you're not just building a business; you're forming a movement. You're engaged in an activity that excites you into action you otherwise would never have taken.

When you work from a place of passion, you will see rewards. Some will be financial. Others will pay dividends in beauty and satisfaction. We're all professionals here. But money will only push you so far. Unless you're a wealthaholic, a lot eventually becomes enough. Even mercenaries have their limits. All our research says that the motivational power of money diminishes dramatically beyond certain thresholds.

Passion for your cause is passion that is inexhaustible. If you have enough commitment to something, there is no barrier you won't break through. Passion is the secret sauce of people who win against all odds. It's the essential force that enables us to cope with the heartache, fatigue and fear that come with any great endeavour.

Ralph Lauren

As one of the world's most recognized fashion icons, Ralph Lauren epitomizes the American penchant for reinvention. He is also a model of vitality. At the age of 76, he still personally directs his brand's new fashion offerings every season. Here's how he describes his passion for the cause in his own words:

> "The best pleasure is the creativity, the stretching, not accepting the ordinary. You want greatness? You have to put the time into greatness. You can't have greatness overnight and you can't have greatness just because you snap your fingers. When you start a collection from the beginning it's the most painful thing in the world because you don't know where you're going. I worry as if it was day one. I say to myself, 'did I do the right thing, did I dig deep enough into my creativity to come up with something new or am I settling for something that feels good to me?'
>
> Fashion is about change. It's about youth. It's about aspiration. It's about what's going on in the world. It's the blend of all things that are happening coming from many different directions.
>
> I can only design into a world filled with women. I see the woman and then I say, 'ok, how does she live, what is she doing, what is she wearing, are they racy, are they intellectual, are they Bohemian, are they European, are they very American?'
>
> Doing the women's collection you've got to pull from your toes because it's truly a ground up restoration of a world. You you've got to create something and make it new every season.

The concepts of how it gets presented both in the music and in the showroom and in its shapes and on the woman becomes a total art piece to me.

Part of the excitement is breaking rules. Knowing the rules and breaking the rules and making them maybe better. The creative moment of reaching higher and higher and dreaming in the middle of turmoil. It all comes together really the night before the show. This goes on. No matter how much in advance you work, no matter how many days you do it, it comes together at three o'clock in the morning, you're finished and it's happened to me for 30 years, doing the same thing.

This is not a job. This is a joy. This is what I breathe. It's what I live. And I think if I cut that off I'd be cutting part of my soul. …"

Diana Nyad

In 2013, on her fifth attempt and at age 64, Diana Nyad became the first person to swim from Cuba to Florida without the aid of a shark cage, swimming 100 miles from Havana to Key West in 53 hours. Her actions demonstrated her commitment to personal growth, irrespective of age, "I am willing to put myself through anything," she says, "temporary pain or discomfort means nothing to me as long as I can see that the experience will take me to a new level. I am interested in the unknown and the only path to the unknown is through breaking barriers, an often-painful process."

Passion for the passage.

My passion is getting people to believe in their capacity to be the best in the world. I want to help people overcome their innate self-doubt. I want to help people stop underestimating their personal power. It breaks my heart when I see people step down because they don't believe they can step up. I hate seeing people ascribe strengths to others that they wish they had when, in fact, they do. On the other hand, I love seeing people vanquish their personal demons just like Princess Five-Weapons.

I am willing to do whatever it takes to help people unleash their inner champions. I'll put everything on the line. That's why I came to Canada in 2001 and launched Environics/Lipkin together with the Environics Research Group. I was 43 with no track record or experience as a professional speaker in Canada.

> **"Mountains can only be surmounted by winding paths."** Goethe

In hindsight, my way here seems stranger than Spielberg-inspired fiction. Like so many people, my journey has led me to my personal hell and back. As a mentor once shared with me, "Be kind to others because everyone is fighting a battle that you know nothing about."

Once upon a time, a wise woman asked a younger one, "Where are all your scars from?" She replied, "They're battle wounds." The older woman asked, "Who were you battling?" The younger woman thought for a while and replied, "myself."

As I share my story with others, I've discovered that my "bizarre" is others' "so what?" Almost everyone I have interviewed over the past decade has a version of the "journey they never thought they would take." As they narrate their history, they shake their heads in wonder and awe, especially because it all turned out the way it did. As the Danish philosopher, Søren Kierkegaard, said, "life can only be understood backwards, but it must be lived forwards."The secret is to remember this truth as you go forward.

I was raised as a white child in an Apartheid South Africa. I grew up being acutely aware of injustice, but I did very little about it. I voted liberal. I donated money. I said the right things to the right people. I led a middle-class life as a marketing executive. I married. In 1984, we had twin children – a boy and a girl. Then in 1987, we immigrated to Toronto, Canada. I joined a large advertising agency, Ogilvy & Mather and I prospered for the first two years. It all seemed to be going according to plan.

Then in 1989, I made a bad real estate investment. I bought high and sold low. The impact didn't cripple me financially but it did debilitate me emotionally. I discovered how fragile I really was. All the fears that lay dormant during my first 30 years sprang to life. I doubted my judgment. I lamented my stupidity. I blamed others. I raged at myself. I lost perspective. I lost my power. I lost my job. I lost my health and I almost lost my wife.

I struggled through the next two years, lurching from one breakdown to the next. I was hospitalized for depression twice. Eventually, towards the end of 1991, we made the decision to go back to South Africa. So I returned home, crushed by how far I thought I had fallen. Four years before, I was the guy most likely to succeed. Now I was the guy most likely to keep on failing.

Within four months of returning, I met a psychiatrist called Bernard Levinson who immediately prescribed a drastic treatment – electro convulsive therapy. He assured me it was safe and promised to take personal care of me. I immediately agreed. I felt so broken that nothing could be worse than where I was. To quote J.K. Rowling, "rock bottom became the solid foundation on which I rebuilt my life."

The impact was miraculous. Within days of the treatment, I regained my mental clarity, my physical vitality and my joie de vivre. The fog lifted just in time for me to participate in one of the great social revolutions in history. What happened over the next decade in South Africa eclipsed my boldest aspirations.

In 1993, I co-authored a book on South Africa's future with Reg Lascaris, a leading advertising executive. We called it "Revelling in the Wild – Business Lessons Out of Africa." As two extreme optimists, we went against the flow by predicting a series of highly favourable trends over the next three years. All of them materialized. We were prescient and lucky in equal measure. To us they were obvious. To many of our fellow countrymen, they were pipedreams.

In May 1994, South Africa became a democracy and Nelson Mandela became its first freely elected president. South Africa became a model of racial reconciliation and a social laboratory to the world. International money flowed into the country and South Africa reclaimed its place in the international community. It may not have been the promised-land but it became a land of great promise.

The spirit of the times was expressed by the TRC - Truth and Reconciliation Commission. The Truth and Reconciliation Commission (TRC) was a court-like body assembled in South Africa after the end of Apartheid. Anybody who felt he or she had been a victim of violence could come forward and be heard at the TRC. Perpetrators of violence could also give testimony and request amnesty from prosecution. The encounters between perpetrators and victims were televised daily. Over 7000 cases were heard. Almost 1000 perpetrators received amnesty. The process opened up a dialogue of discovery and forgiveness.

As Desmond Tutu, the TRC chairman, said at the time, "There is no situation that is not transfigurable. There is no situation that is devoid of hope. There are no ordinary people in my theology. It is the small people, the ones who used to be nonentities, who are the stars. When you forgive someone, you abandon your right to revenge. On the other hand, it is only by confessing that you can open yourself up to the possibility of being forgiven and begin to work towards the restoration of the relationship. Forgiveness is like opening a window and letting the fresh air in."

This was the context in which the South African narrative evolved over the next six years. Yes, there was ongoing economically motivated crime but it was dwarfed by the ongoing transformation of the entire society. It was the perfect arena for me in my self-appointed role as motivator and high-performance coach to the country. There was a huge appetite to learn and massive opportunities to satisfy that hunger. I co-authored four bestselling books with preeminent local talents and partnered with many others to impact thousands of people.

In 2000, I turned 42 and became restless again. South Africa was still a relatively small market. Its economy is one fifth of the Canadian economy and just two percent of the American economy. I also wanted to conquer my own personal nemesis and see if I could succeed where I had failed so dramatically before. I had something to prove and I wanted to prove it in the most competitive, lucrative market on the planet – North America.

So in 2001, I returned to Canada. Ten years had passed since my previous tenure. Almost no one remembered me. No one cared what had happened in the distant past. I was free to reinvent myself in my re-adopted land. But I had learned one key lesson during the decade I had been away: partnership is the key to the magic kingdom. Talent is temporary; teams endure. I would achieve nothing without the impetus of extraordinary allies.

One morning in late 2000, during a visit to Canada, I read an article by Michael Adams, the founder and CEO of the Environics Research Group. It focused on the twelve "Values Tribes" that Adams and his teams of pollsters had described in his provocatively titled book, Sex in the Snow. It highlighted the momentum of Canadians towards the "lower right quadrant" comprising a blend of idealism, self-belief and quest for fulfilment. It spoke of social values like "Adaptive Navigation" and "Personal Creativity." It introduced me to the concept of "heterarchy" which is the opposite of hierarchy. In a heterarchy, leaders and followers are interchangeable depending on circumstances. The model is fluid and dynamic, designed to go with the flow, not protect and defend.

It was as though Adams and his team had defined and quantified my intuitive thoughts. As I completed the article, I decided to call him and suggest a joint venture: in return for access to the insights and a place in his enterprise, I would build a motivational practice that would "democratize the data." I would use the Environics research to help thousands of Canadians and Americans understand how to thrive in their changing environment.

Michael Adams co-founded Environics in 1970. From a start-up focused on public affairs polling, Environics has grown to become a leading market research firm employing experts in a range of practice areas from pharmaceuticals and financial services to human resources and consumer marketing.

In the 1980s, Environics introduced the North American marketplace to the Social Values research method, first developed at the renowned Cofremca in Paris. With questions drawn from the fields of social psychology and sociology and an emphasis on segmenting respondents into groups of like-minded peers, this rich and innovative methodology has helped hundreds of top companies understand their customers and employees more deeply and tailor their communications to connect with their stakeholders' core values.

I met with Adams in November 2000 over a long lunch at Pangaea Restaurant in downtown Toronto. In between glasses of Chablis and Cabernet, we established an immediate rapport. Adams is a born raconteur who loves nothing more than to turn data into stories. He is also a mentor and sponsor of emerging talent. I pitched him my ideas to start a motivational practice to complement his existing businesses. He immediately accepted with a smile and another toast to our future good fortune.

I spent the first half of 2001 transforming a group of select Social Values into a high performance program called, "Your Personal

Best – Twelve Personal Best Practices To Help You Live At Your Highest Level." It was launched in October 2001 and immediately took off.

The market loved the formula of inspirational, actionable insights drawn from sound, empirical data. Over the next five years, I published three bestselling books on sales, communication and leadership. By 2006, I was among the top twenty motivational speakers in North America, earning over $2 million a year in speaking fees. The fusion of South African mojo with Canadian know-how was an irresistible offering and the timing was impeccable.

In a post 9-11 world, my global citizenship resonated with a range of decision makers who wanted to cross-pollinate their people's perspective. I was new. I was disruptive. I had an endless flow of data points from my colleagues at Environics. And I was over 40. This was my third and final act. I had to make it work.

I also aligned myself with a leading seminar company called "The Power Within." Three to four times a year, this company would feature me as the lead-off speaker at mega-sessions that attracted over 5000 delegates. I lived for the kudos and affirmation of those moments. Laughter and applause are my favourite sounds. What's more, delegates at those events would often invite to speak at their companies. My phone rang perpetually and I delivered up to 150 engagements a year.

Momentum is a beautiful thing until it stops. And that's what happened at the end of 2008 with the onset of the "Great Recession." The market for high paid "keynote speakers" declined dramatically. Elaborate corporate meetings were scaled back as companies desperately tried to shore up their shaky finances. Even companies that were financially sound wanted to avoid the optics of spending money on "luxuries" while they were laying off people. Speakers who previously charged $25,000 a speech were willing to talk for $5000-$10,000.

There is an African proverb that states,

> **"When the waterhole gets smaller, the animals get meaner."**

As the market shrank, the competition intensified. Although I continued to introduce new programs, I felt like I had become just another competitor scrambling to survive another day. Like thousands of other entrepreneurs, I questioned my philosophy, my business model and my belief in myself.

As a digital immigrant, I also felt like I was at a disadvantage to all the digital natives invading my space. Clients were asking for experts on social media and CRM (customer relationship management) programs. I sensed I was no longer the innovator and disruptor. I was now the status quo. I was the representative of the old model – the classic motivational speaker, albeit with sound data to support his claims. My phone rang less frequently.

In 2009 and 2010, I lost my sense of personal entitlement. I stopped believing I would automatically win an assignment simply because I was available to do it. My personal identity as a sure-fire winner morphed into someone less sure of myself. I approached each prospect with more humility and doubt. I questioned my raison d'être. I asked myself repeatedly, "What can I bring to this client that no one else can?" Often, my response was, "I don't know."But as Napoleon Hill, the great motivational author, said,

> **"Every adversity, every failure, every heartache carries with it the seed of an equal or greater benefit."**

The advantage of being disillusioned is that the illusions are stripped away. I also felt like Zack Mayo, when he said to Drill Sergeant Foley in An Officer and a Gentleman, "I've got nowhere else to go." There is nothing else that I wanted to do. I lived to speak and I spoke to live. The conversation itself was the reward.

I went from wanting to win the game, to wanting to just stay in the game. I have learned that, no matter how good you are, you are going to experience natural ebbs and flows. No one can always be on. There is a season for everything. I also learned that if you can stay in the game long enough, you can figure out a way to win it again. Past performance is a guide to future success. Adaptation, resilience and ingenuity can grow stronger with age. If you embrace your new realities, your new realities will eventually embrace you.

As the market rebounded in 2011, so did the call for HEROes – Highly Experienced Resourceful Operators. The Great Recession highlighted the need for talent that stood the test of time. The cool heads that prevailed over the previous three years were also now tinged with grey or sparsely covered. It became cool to be 50-something, especially if you're fit and vibrant.

I also had something in 2011 that I didn't have in 2001: a track record and loyal base of strong Mike Lipkin advocates. To my great gratitude, I discovered hundreds of people trusted my judgment and were willing to pay for more of it. My business evolved from pure motivational speaking to personal coaching, corporate strategizing, video production and customized high-performance programs.

Apple, YouTube and LinkedIn enabled me to scale my impact. I learned how to create simple videos on my iPhone and upload them to YouTube. My vast network on LinkedIn enabled me to stay in constant contact with thousands of carefully selected key decision-makers. My cadre of partners in web-design, publishing, conference development, training and leadership introduced me to a whole new level of opportunities. Environics also recalibrated its flagship Social Values Monitor to make it even more impactful.

By 2012, I had emerged from the crisis with a renewed sense of power and purpose. I wasn't the new kid on the block, but I believed I had something even more alluring: the cachet of sustained success. I discovered that *New-and-Improved* could compete with *Totally New* and win.

Get busy living

There are *millennials*. And then there are *perennials* – people who defy conventional definitions of age and stay forever young.

That's me. In 2015, I delivered 110 talks on top of an array of other motivational pursuits. The momentum is back and I'm fuelling it with everything I have.

Things get harder as we grow older. Our natural elasticity becomes more brittle; our recovery time takes longer; robust health isn't automatic; and the natural charisma of youth has elapsed. On the other hand, if we manage it well, our authority increases. We have a better handle on what's important. We manage our resources more efficiently. We become more generous. Our horizons are wider so we can see further. We also become happier. Beyond 40, there is a direct positive correlation between age and contentment.

According to The Economist Magazine (December 16, 2010):
"People, studies show, behave differently at different ages. Older people have fewer rows and come up with better solutions to conflict. They are better at controlling their emotions, better at accepting misfortune and less prone to anger. In one study, for instance, subjects were asked to listen to recordings of people supposedly saying disparaging things about them. Older and younger people were similarly saddened, but older people less angry and less inclined to pass judgment, taking the view, as one put it, that 'you can't please all the people all the time.'"

In our 50s, we need to make *The Simple Choice*. To quote the great Andy Dufresne in The Shawshank Redemption, "It comes down to a simple choice, get busy living or get busy dying." We increase our engagement with life or we begin to disengage. We prepare to scale the next peak or we sound the retreat. With a realistic life expectancy of 30 more years, our choice has enormous consequences. According to the Environics Social Values Research, only 40 percent of 50-plus somethings have made the choice to fully engage with the rest of their life. We call them the Connected Enthusiasts and the Autonomous Rebels. They are social and ambitious in equal measure. They live the Steve Jobs mantra, "Stay hungry, stay foolish."

This book is how I'm getting busy living. It's my declaration of commitment to my cause.

I CAN THRIVE UNDER ANY CIRCUMSTANCES

Champions have a core value that endows them with a sense of personal invincibility. It's called *Adaptive Navigation*. It's the conviction they can adapt to any situation and navigate through it. They find a way or make a way, especially when others say there is no way.

Champions have a built in GPS system that directs them where they need to go wherever they are. There's no such thing as being "lost" any more. There are just different routes to your goal. You never have to fear not reaching your destination. Sometimes it may just take a little longer. But there's one big caveat here: you have to have a goal that's big enough to register on the global satellite system. Small goals don't guide you very far.

Another word for champion is "denizen." Say it aloud: denizen. It's as decisive as it sounds. A denizen is someone who feels at home anywhere in the world. They're super charged, global citizens. Wherever they find themselves, that's where they belong. They're never misplaced. They radiate a sense of ease and wellbeing.

They take control of their environment by going with the flow. They see through cultural veneers to the beating hearts within.

A denizen's chief asset is her ingenuity. She's cleverly inventive and original. Everything around her becomes a tool to enhance her odds and achieve her goals. Along the way, she enables others to stretch because people are her chief resource.

A denizen knows that every meeting changes its participants in some way. We're all the sum of all our interactions with others. The smallest touch can make the biggest impression. The kindness of strangers may be more transformative than the generosity of good friends.

That's why I love to travel. Every moment becomes a melting pot of cultures and interaction. In the last year, I have been to 10 countries including Thailand, Greece, Spain, South Africa, England, Mexico, Dubai, Italy and Switzerland. Most these trips have been on business where my mission was consistent across the globe. The champions shine through, irrespective of ethnicity or nationality. They speak a language that transcends language – it's called results. They make things happen no matter what else is happening.

DHL

DHL is a global express logistics company. They brand themselves as, "The Most International Company in the World." They have operations in 220 countries. They pride themselves on being first in and last out of the most troubled hotspots. Their unique value proposition is that everyone at DHL is a CIS – a Certified International Specialist. The CIS program provides training on the fundamentals of international shipping, ensuring every employee, regardless of their role in the company, is equipped to consult customers on successful cross-border delivery. Their mindset transcends geography. The only thing that matters is the successful facilitation of international trade. Their self-imposed mandate is to help their customers thrive under any circumstances.

However, you don't have to travel far for your world to change. Just staying where you are can transport you to a new reality. My world today is nothing like it was even a year ago. The clients are new. The projects are new. The media is new. Even the roles I'm playing are new. Unfamiliar is my new familiar and I'll bet it's the same for you.

Champions don't bank on things getting easier. They bank on themselves getting better.

As I write these words, the world is entering a new phase of mega-uncertainty. The headwinds are increasing. Growth is flat lining. There are no safe havens. Greece is codeword for failure. China's growth engine is spluttering. Canada is struggling. And the US is experiencing major turbulence in an election year. However, as Baron Rothschild, an 18th century British nobleman and banker, said, "The time to buy is when the blood runs in the streets, even if it is your own." He should know. Rothschild made a fortune buying in the panic that followed the Battle of Waterloo against Napoleon.

In his book, Great by Choice, Jim Collins states,

> "10Xers (companies beating their industry indexes by a minimum of 10 times over 15 years) differ from their less successful comparisons in how they maintain hyper-vigilance in good times as well as bad. Even in calm, clear, positive conditions, 10Xers constantly consider the possibility that

> events could turn against them at any moment. Indeed, they believe that conditions will – absolutely, with 100 percent certainty – turn against them without warning, at some unpredictable point in time, at some highly inconvenient moment. And they'd better be prepared."

Martin Luther King said, "The ultimate measure of a man is not where he stands in moments of comfort and convenience, but where he stands at times of challenge and controversy." Today, comfort and convenience are rare states of being. In fact, comfort is antithetical to being a champion. Becoming the best in the world and thriving in adversity is anything but comfortable. And it certainly isn't convenient. Being able to thrive in any circumstances means being comfortable with discomfort.

A life without threat is no life at all. Freedom from fear isn't freedom from hazards, trials, challenges, competitors and crises. Preparing for them is. That's how we build the muscle to turn threats into opportunities.

The threat of depression is always there as a presence for me. Knowing it's out there keeps me vigilant. I walk the line between breaking through and breaking down. Too much hubris is as damaging as too much humility. It's about finding the balance between animation and reserve, determination and discretion, action and stillness. Sometimes I still have to go too far to find out how far I can go. But that's how I test my limits. All the opportunities are in the discomfort zone.

As the folks at The North Face say, "Never stop exploring." Even when you stumble in the search for breakthroughs, you still move forward. There are no failures, only unexpected results that can be repurposed later. Every experience is a deposit on a future contribution. As a speaker, my greatest thrill is a standing ovation. Nothing is more rewarding than a group of accomplished professionals rising together to acknowledge my excellence. Those are the moments that make everything else worthwhile.

Here's the really scary thing about my role: the audience always expects to be wowed. They expect the inspiration to play big and live large. They expect a performance that entertains and enables them to surpass their limits. Anything short of spectacular will fall short of my clients' expectations. In pursuing success, I set myself up for failure because it's impossible to shoot the lights out every time.

I do all I can to prepare for preeminence: I do my homework. I work out before my talk; I visualize success; I chant my mantras; I reaffirm my belief in my ability and my faith in a power greater than me. But every now and then, I feel like the gods of motivation forsake me. My delivery isn't instinctive. The thoughts and words seemed bottlenecked somewhere in my brain. The audience appears to sense my inner ordeal. I don't connect with them on a visceral level. An hour lasts forever. The talk ends and the applause is superficial.

It gets worse from there – especially if I have travelled to deliver the program. I do a postmortem of the experience – I think of all the things I shouldn't have said or done. I think of all the ways I could have improved it. I think of all the expectations I fell short of. Then I resolve never to slip up like that again. I think about how I could have improved my performance. I register my lessons learned where it hurts the most.

Those moments are vital for me. They make me feel like a beginner all over again. My complacency is shattered. My ego is crushed. But I'm like the anti-Humpty-Dumpty: Mike Lipkin sat on the wall; Mike Lipkin had a slight fall; all of his clients and all of his friends put him back quickly together again. Learning to live with what you fear most is the antidote to fear itself.

The miracle is that I hit a home run 99 times out of 100. I'm the Barry Bonds of my business (without the steroids). But when I'm mediocre, I have to be careful not to beat myself up. In a world filled with superlatives, passable must sometimes suffice. The audience forgets about it almost instantly, but I carry it around a lot longer. And my bet is so do you. It's only human. But resilience is a function of how quickly you can forget your defeats. The trick is to hold onto them only as long as it takes to extract the learning from them. Otherwise, you take your defeats into the next game and that guarantees another loss.

In the African wild, the cheetah is one of nature's most skilled predators. It can reach speeds of over 50 miles an hour. And yet, the cheetah misses its prey half the time. Every time it hunts, it expects to eat. A miss is simply a reason to try again and again until it succeeds. You'll never see a cheetah sitting under a tree dreaming of being a vegetarian. Self-pity is not part of its emotional repertoire. Neither is frustration. As D.H. Lawrence wrote, "I never saw a wild thing sorry for itself. A small bird will drop frozen dead from a bough without ever having felt sorry for itself."

If you want to be good, you have to be willing to be bad.
We can plan for all the variables but we cannot control all the variables. Just one discordant element can disrupt the harmony. If you're a pro with pride, you'll prevent a disaster almost all of the

time. But to a pro with pride, even a B+ performance is a disaster. I've seen people lambaste themselves mercilessly even though they did the best they could in the circumstances.

No matter who we are, we are imperfect beings in search of perfect results. If you've done all you can, you should expect to get all you want. But you should also be prepared to come up empty. Otherwise, you'll experience a sense of entitlement that is both arrogant and self-defeating. Whenever I go through an attack of hubris (that's when I think I can do no wrong), I slip, stumble and fall. It's always a shock. I feel like retreating quietly or protesting loudly. Then I remember it's not what happened that is crushing. It's my interpretation of what happened. Nothing means anything except the meaning we give it.

Perfect is achievable but it's fleeting. It's when everything goes exactly the way we want it to go. In fact, the biggest rush for me is when clients tell me, "That went exactly as planned." I'm amazed that those moments happen as often as they do. But when they don't, I accept them as inevitable. It still hurts but not as deep or as long.

In the movie Rocky Balboa, Rocky says to his son, "You, me or nobody is going to hit as hard as life. But it ain't about how hard you're hit, it is about how hard you can get hit and keep moving forward, how much can you take and keep moving forward. That's how winning is done!" Ain't that the truth? Being stoppable is a luxury you cannot afford. You can pursue perfection but sometimes you have to be okay with being merely passable.

The spectre of a merely passable performance haunts many stars. For the majority of C-suite players I coach, the pain of losing is greater than the joy of winning. Joy seems temporary but pain lasts a very long time. It's perpetuated in their minds by their constant cognition. The more they think about the experience, the more things they find to obsess about. Avoiding embarrassment is as strong as any other force driving them.

Unless you have the bliss of a monk, it may not be possible to entirely banish thoughts of embarrassment from your mind. In a world where so much depends on social currency, other people's opinions of us are crucial to our wellbeing. But it's possible to live with these thoughts, knowing that we create them. In fact, other people may not even remember what happened. Or even if they do, it's not nearly as important to them as it was to you. You are not the centre of other people's universes, they are.

Being a champion is a direct function of how effectively you can neutralize your fear of embarrassment.

At some point, we all get found out. We will all underperform in a clutch moment, especially when we've consistently over delivered on others' expectations of us in the past. It comes with the territory. The greater our stature, the harder we fall.

Embarrassment is the flip side to differentiation. Being special means putting yourself in a space where others aren't prepared to go. That statement alone sets one apart from the pack. It's delicious when it works and ugly when it doesn't. Success is the premium we earn for risking embarrassment.

Here's the ultimate tradeoff: either we risk an instant of embarrassment or a lifetime of regret. The pain of embarrassment is never as bad as the fear of embarrassment. But the pain of regret is the worst pain of all. It's frustration, self-anger and personal loss all rolled into one. So the next time you're tempted to wimp out, anticipate the price you'll pay in tears. Then step up with a smile. If you finish what you start, you win personal gold no matter what the external result.

The saddest word in the English language is "almost." The two saddest words in the English language are "if only." The three saddest words are "I should have." The four saddest words are "I could have been." The five saddest words are "it is too late now."

In all my years as a motivator and coach, I've never spoken to anyone who was crushed by embarrassment. Bruised maybe, but broken? Never. But I know many people who are heartbroken because they didn't seize the opportunity when it was within their grasp. Carpe diem or complain forever. It's your call.

When you are scared of being hurt, turn to the King, the Warrior, the Magician or the Lover for help.

Once upon a time, in a land far away, there lived an evil man who delighted in making others angry and miserable. He was a wealthy man who had made his money through the tears and sweat of others. Every day he went out into the streets and insulted all those around him. He would only stop when he had made someone cry or lose his temper. He never failed to upset or anger a person. He revelled in his reputation as a bully who was feared by many.

At the same time in this land, there was a wise and gentle man who helped everyone with their problems. This wise man had a reputation for never losing his temper. He was known never to raise his voice, even in the direst circumstances. He was a source of comfort and inspiration to hundreds of people.

Of course, when the evil man heard about the wise man, he became determined to make him angry so that he would lose his temper and his composure. The evil man travelled to see the wise man. When he arrived in front of the wise man, he proceeded to hurl abuse at him. He insulted the wise man's religion, his family, his culture and his friends. On and on he continued. For an entire hour, he bombarded the wise man with all the rudest, crudest insults he could think of.

Eventually, when the evil man had temporarily run out of invectives, the wise man asked the evil man a question. In a calm, considered voice, he asked, "Tell me, sir. If someone offers you a gift and you refuse to accept the gift, to whom does the gift belong?" The evil man immediately responded by shouting, "What a stupid question. Obviously the gift belongs to the person who is offering the gift!" The wise man just smiled and said, "Well, then sir, if I refuse to accept your abuse, to whom does it belong?"

The fear of being hurt, humiliated or rejected by another person is the single biggest bogeyman for many people I speak to. All that has to happen as we grow up is for a single person to ridicule us. If this person was influential - a teacher, parent, older brother or sister, friend - it can scar us forever. Sticks and stones can break our bones, but words hurt us deeply. For many of us, the wound remains so painful that we never risk embarrassment again. To paraphrase Henry David Thoreau, we live lives of quiet desperation. We want to speak out, but we are afraid to stand up.

Every day I talk to people who permit themselves to be defined by others. They let other people live rent free in their minds.

On Planet Earth, you cannot go back in time. You can't erase the hurts; the abuse, the disrespect, the insults. But you can validate yourself now. You can stand tall. You can be a King, a Warrior, a Magician or a Lover. Or you can be all four of them, depending on your circumstances.

The King, the Warrior, the Magician and the Lover are the four general archetypes. According to the great psychiatrist, Carl Jung, an archetype is a universal idea or model that exists within all of us. For the vast majority of us, probably including you, these archetypes exist unconsciously. That is, until now. So let's explore the four archetypes and how they can help you.

The King (or Queen) stands tall. He looks people in the eye. He is very still. He is not aggressive. He doesn't throw his weight around. He doesn't have to; he knows his power. He is gentle.

The Warrior meets troubles head on. She is unafraid to face whatever challenges come her way. But she is not aggressive. Whereas the King stands still, the Warrior moves. She goes out to meet the challenge.

The Magician is intuitive, lateral thinking, a helper. He reaches out. People talk to him. He is the shaman or the South African tradition, the traditional healer known as the sangoma.

The Lover is not the sexy, horny, testosterone-driven Don Juan. The Lover is highly sensitive. He reads people. He loves the act of loving. He supports and comforts. He loves to connect with others just for the pleasure of intimacy.

All of us have a dominant archetype that drives us. I am a Magician. When the situation demands it, though, I can be a King, Warrior or a Lover.

My point here is that you have the resources to call on your King, Warrior, Magician or Lover whenever you need to. But you also need the awareness and flexibility to play the archetypes effectively. For example, the King at work must be a Lover and Magician at home. Or the Lover at home may need to be the Warrior at work. Flex with the situation, Go with the flow.

So from today, be a King, Warrior, Magician or Lover. But never be a slave to other people's dysfunctions or flaws. No matter where you've been, there's no limit to where you can go. Give yourself the chance. You've got some powerful champions within you. Use them.

MY BEST DAYS ARE ALWAYS AHEAD OF ME

Jeff Bezos, CEO of Amazon, says, "It's always day one."

The future begins here and it begins now. No matter how old you are, your best days are ahead of you by virtue of the very fact that they're ahead of you. Yesterdays are history. Tomorrows are imaginary. Today is our stage, our laboratory, our studio, our factory and our playground, all rolled into one.

Our current level of happiness is a direct function of what we expect will happen next. We create our future by what we do today. Yet what we do today is influenced by our expectations of tomorrow. I can only write these words because I expect them to be read. I expect to share them through videos and seminars around the world. I expect them to help others become champions. I expect it all. That's why I'm giving it my all.

Hope is a strategy because it's the source of everything else. I have never met a pessimistic champion. No matter where they've been, they expect their future to be better. That's what drives them forward. Sometimes their belief is based on fact and sometimes it's self-created fiction. But it's self-fulfilling. We act according to our view of the future.

It's easy to believe that your best days are ahead of you at the beginning of your career. It takes a conscious will to still believe it as you mature along the way. Half of the entire workforce is over the age of 45. And according to Gallup, a leading research company, less than a third of people are engaged at work. Professional engagement means having passion about what they do and being committed to producing great work. What's more, after six months on the job, rates of engagement tend to fall off sharply. Workers are typically more engaged in their first six months (52 percent) on the job than they will be at any other stage in their employment with that company.

Gallup also found that only 41 percent of employees felt that they know what their company stands for and what makes its brand different from its competitors' brands. So it's not surprising people lose their passion for their work so quickly.

At most of the organizations I work with the biggest challenge is inspiring experienced staff-members to raise their game to the level demanded by the new realities. There's a direct correlation between length of experience and cynicism about the future. The longer you have been in a workplace, the harder it is to be happy about being there. The pressure to perform is intensifying at the same time that people's personal intensity is declining. "I'm getting too old for this" is the lament of the middle-aged worker.

Across all demographics, Gallup's research shows that focusing on "opportunity to do best" and "mission and purpose" are the strongest factors for engaging employees. Businesses scoring in the top half on employee engagement nearly doubled their odds of success compared with those in the bottom half.

Gallup has found that building employees' strengths is a far more effective approach than trying to improve weaknesses. However, even those managers who focused on employees' weaknesses cut their active disengagement in half. Those who focused on their employees' strengths doubled their engagement scores. Teams that focus on their strengths every day have 12.5 percent greater productivity. There's also a direct correlation between employees' engagement levels and their physical health. Employees thriving in overall wellbeing have 41 percent lower health-related costs compared with employees who are struggling.

The irony is it's harder being disillusioned and cynical than committed and optimistic. Anxiety is an inside job that multiplies fatigue and overwhelm. The perennials that are getting better with age understand anticipation is nine tenths of success or failure. Anticipation of Armageddon is a cue to retreat into a personal bunker and wait for the cataclysm to pass. Anticipation of the next breakthrough is the signal to accelerate our learning and precipitate positive change.

Right here, right now, make the decision to engage strongly. Act as though your best days are ahead of you and you will become your own self-fulfilling prophecy. If you're reading this, you're still in the game. Decide to be in the game to win. Swing for the fences. Expect to hit home runs. But also expect to strike out. One thing is certain; you'll get on base a lot more times. And as Billy Beane, the legendary manager of the Oakland A's baseball team, said, "You get on base, we win. You don't, we lose. And I hate losing." Beane discovered that a player's on-base percentage, how often he reached a base, is the greatest predictor of the team's probability of winning.

Danny Meyer

Danny Meyer is a 57-year-old restaurant impresario who founded and runs the Union Square Hospitality Group, which comprises nine restaurants in New York City. He is also the founder and largest shareholder of Shake Shack, a chain of casual eateries that went public in 2015. His net worth is estimated to be close to $500 million. He states, "I'm constantly inspired by travel. The opportunity to learn how people from other cultures live, eat, relate to each other and express themselves fuels my imagination unimaginably." Meyer's goal is to make diners feel at home, only better. He says, "We're going to do some fun stuff that makes you say, 'I never knew home was quite this nice.'" Meyer's conviction that his best days are always ahead of him inspires him to make it a self-fulfilling prophecy.

Kim Yost

Earlier, I mentioned my client and mentor, Kim Yost. He is president of Art Van, a leading chain of furniture stores based in Warren, Michigan. At the beginning of each year, Kim and his team think about the kind of company that could come into their market and make them obsolete. He thinks about their product, their brands, their infrastructure and their people. He thinks about how they will market their offering and what value-add they will bring to customers.

Kim conjures up a model of this hypothetical new competitor that scares him into action to make his business look exactly like that. As the leader, Kim asks himself, "What is the chairman and the board looking for? What are customers looking for? Who could replace me?" Once he understands what's required, he becomes the person he needs to replace himself with.

Kim has achieved five years of double-digit compound growth in a tough market. He claims it's all about killing the parts that don't serve him and feeding the parts that do – because his best days are always ahead of him.

What would you do today if you knew for certain your best days are always ahead of you? How much more excitement would you feel? How much more happiness would you spread around you?

However old you are right now, it's the right age to take action on your dream. Nelson Mandela was 69 when he became the first democratically elected president of South Africa. Ronald Reagan was the same age when he became the oldest newly elected president in American history. Harlan Saunders was 66 when he started Kentucky Fried Chicken. Ray Kroc was 54 when he started

McDonalds. The great actress, Dame Helen Mirren, is peaking in her late 60s. At 71, Keith Richard has just produced his first album in 23 years. At the age of 97, Herman Wouk published his 25th book, The Law Giver, still dreaming of returning to the best-seller list that he dominated for so long.

Speaking of dreams, let's begin now…

I DREAM LIKE A CHAMPION

I DREAM BIG

I SHARE MY DREAM

MY DREAM IS ATTACHED TO A DEADLINE

MY DREAM STRETCHES ME TO DO MORE

MY DREAM UPLIFTS OTHERS TO ACHIEVE THEIR DREAM

I DREAM LIKE A CHAMPION

You can attract your own eland just by thinking about it. If you dream about it while you're awake, it will cross your path. You have the magic. Use it. Or lose it.

Lourens Van der Post

Lourens Van der Post, the great author and anthropologist, tells of his experience with the Bushmen of the Kalahari. The Bushmen are great hunters and Van der Post once sat with them before they set off on a hunt. On this occasion, they drew a picture of the eland – a large buck prized for its abundance of meat – on a rock. They confronted the rock and said to the painted image, "We're going to come and fetch you now."

Van der Post invited them to hunt the eland in his jeep but they refused. They preferred to run alongside it for two whole days.

Eventually they discovered the spoor of the eland, tracked it and killed it. After they had put the animal in the jeep, he said to them, "I'm sure that back home, your families will be very pleased to know that you have killed an eland." They looked at him and replied, "Our families already know. We've told them with our hearts." Van der Post just smiled and shook his head in amusement. As they approached the camp, however, he saw that the women were already doing the dance of the eland. The Bushmen had the ability to communicate their energy and thoughts from a distance.

In fact, we all have this ability. It's just because our minds are cluttered by the noise of the lives we lead, we think we've lost this ability. But it's never lost. It's built in. We call it luck when we attract good fortune. It's not. It's the linkage between all of us. It's the instinct inside us that we have forgotten about.

We've busied ourselves into another way of living. We have magic inside that we don't even begin to use. The people we regard as lucky are people who, consciously or unconsciously, are using this magic to attract their personal elands. They have the aura. They know they're not lucky. They just know that they know. They're guided. They're not forcing it. They're flowing through it. All the time they're sharpening this skill. They're developing it. They're growing more magical. Are you?

As I write these words, I have painted the image of this book being sold in tens of thousands on the canvas of my mind. I dream about the thousands of people around the world that this book will help. I know that you're reading these words because of the dreams I've had and the images I've painted on my mental rock.

So today, begin sending out your energy. Think deeply about the people you want to connect with. Transmit your love and good wishes to them now. Dream about your personal eland. What do you really want that will nurture your family and your community? Paint or draw it on a rock, a wall, a piece of paper, anywhere. Now. Or if you prefer to describe your painting in words, write down your vision. Call to it from the depths of your personal power. Believe you have the magic to attract it to you. Make sure that what you want will really help those around you. And don't stop. If you can dream it, you can do it.

> **"Those who dream by day are cognizant of many things which escape those who dream only by night."** Edgar Allan Poe

A dream is literally a series of images, thoughts or emotions that pass through our minds while asleep. Sometimes they're highly pleasurable and sometimes they're nightmares. We can wake up feeling wondrous. Or we can wake up feeling like we've just escaped from Alcatraz. The point is the dreams we experience while asleep are involuntary. They're the realm of the mysterious and the unconscious. While they can be analyzed, they cannot be designed.

There is another kind of dream. It's the series of images, thoughts or emotions that pass through our minds while awake. They too can make us feel wondrous. Or they can make us feel like we're locked up in our own prisons. But these dreams are entirely, purposely conscious. They're created at will, accessed at will and acted on at will. These dreams are as real to their creators as anything else they will experience in their lives.

Billy Wilder, the prolific filmmaker and screenwriter, said, "You have to have a dream so you can get up in the morning." Dreams and caffeine go together like white on rice. Without dreams, your imagination isn't animated. Our deepest resources aren't activated. Our enthusiasm isn't aroused. Without dreams, there is no colour, only shades of grey (and not the exciting kind either).

"We are such stuff as dreams are made on," Shakespeare wrote in The Tempest. We are built on dreams and dreams are built on us. Our dreams are as much a part of us as our DNA. They shape our realm of possibility and scope of action. The bigger the dream, the bigger the realm of possibility and the wider the scope of action.

Fact is stranger than fiction. It's strange to me how few people have a big, bold dream that inspires them to do more and be more. As someone who makes a living helping people turn their dreams into reality, I've discovered that the vast majority of people don't have a dream. Don't get me wrong; they want the "American or Canadian Dream." They want to be happy, healthy and free from fear. They want their children to thrive. They want the next promotion or the next vacation. Their dreams come in a box that's been defined by their environment.

When I ask people the simple, direct question, "What's your dream?" I usually get a vague response of something, somewhere, someday, somehow. It's not that they don't want to fulfil their dreams. It's just the need isn't urgent or acute enough. On one hand, they may be happy enough. On the other, they may be too stressed to even contemplate a dream. Their mission may simply be to get through the day. Whatever it is, it isn't a meaningful driver of performance in their life.

"First I throw my mind over the bar and then my body follows,"

Dick Fosbury said just before he won the gold medal at the 1968 Olympics in Mexico with a world record high jump of 7.35 feet. Not only did he set a record, he also defined an entirely new "back first" approach to his sport – The Fosbury Flop. In his mind, Fosbury set the bar where he wanted it to be. Then he surpassed it. What's your bar?

Before you go further, write down your dream for the next year and next five years. Think about your work, your health, your leisure, your family, your community and any other key priority for you. As you think about your dream, think about its power to excite you into action. Do you feel the thrill of "living the dream?" Can you see it in crystal clear, compelling colour? Can you feel your endorphins beginning to pump as you live it live in your mind?

Or is it more prosaic? Is it just "it would be nice?" Is it a kind-of, sort-of, may-be opportunity? Is it more "I have a hope" than "I have a dream?"

I DREAM BIG

After researching and interviewing thousands of champions over the past 23 years, I've discovered one proven, incontestable trait: they have a dream that is big, audacious and urgent. Their dream is like a hunger that needs to be satiated *now*. When they describe their dream, they're describing something that's already happening in their mind. They're so enamored of their dream it accompanies them like a constant presence. It's the unspoken dialogue that underpins their conversations. It's fascinating and magnetic in equal measure because it is so rare.

We all want a part of a champion's dream. They either inspire us to emulate them or to vicariously enjoy their dream. It's like the feeling we experience in great movies about the spirit and the vision of heroes. Think about Chariots of Fire, Unbroken, Gladiator, Beautiful Mind and The Imitation Game to name a few. The difference is champions sustain their passion until it becomes real. Then they start all over again.

There is a language of "Dreaming Big." It's scary, thrilling, rich, engaging, colourful, bright, intense, human, ambitious, indelible, inspiring, electric, humbling, vivid, taut, disruptive, courageous, connective, nourishing and creative. Add your words here.

Some of the most courageous people I know are still too timid. They take on everyday tasks with diligence and care. They face down difficulties and get the job done. But they don't dream big. Either their aspirations are too modest or they simply haven't taken the time to define their dream. When I ask about their dreams, they're always merely a step or two above their current place. Their dreams are puny when they could be powerful. While they still have something to stretch for, they don't have something to reimagine themselves for.

When you dream big, you imagine yourself as someone living the dream. You're bigger than the person you are now. The dream and the person in the dream are part of the same show. It must be worthy of your own Academy Award for best picture, best director, best cast of characters and best screenplay. What would that take for you?

For me, it would take this book reaching over 100,000 people. It would take 600 engagements in the next five years. It would take a global video and audio channel that reaches over a million people. It would take the infusion of my personal content into the vocabularies and mindsets of thousands of people as they become their own **BADASS - Bold Audacious Dreamer And Spectacular Success.**

I'm smiling as I'm writing this because I've just discovered what being a BADASS really is - Bold Audacious Dreamer And Spectacular Success. No one in the world ever knew that until I wrote it. How cool is that?

I have to be a BADASS to help others become a BADASS. If you're reading this, I've succeeded in helping you become a BADASS. But since I'm writing these words before you read them, I have to become a BADASS in advance. The only difference between the person I am now and the person I will be when you read these words is time. As the great actor, Jeremy Irons says, "We all have our time machines. Some take us back, they're called memories. Some take us forward, they're called dreams."

Here are some of my favourite quotes on dreaming big:

> **"In the end, one detail is inarguable: There will always be those searching for treasure. Never forget: We are a country founded on legends and myths. We love them, especially legends of treasure. Looking for treasure isn't just part of being an American, it is America."** Brad Meltzer

"You gotta have a dream. If you don't have a dream, how you gonna make a dream come true?" Oscar Hammerstein II

"New York is the city of dreamers and time and again it's the place where the greatest dream of all, the American dream, has been tested and has triumphed." Michael Bloomberg

"Believe in love. Believe in magic. Hell, believe in Santa Claus. Believe in others. Believe in yourself. Believe in your dreams. If you don't, who will?" Jon Bon Jovi

"I believe in everything until it's disproved. So I believe in fairies, the myths, dragons. It all exists, even if it's in your mind. Who's to say that dreams and nightmares aren't as real as the here and now?" John Lennon

"I have had dreams and I have had nightmares, but I have conquered my nightmares because of my dreams." Jonas Salk

"Let your dreams outgrow the shoes of your expectations." Ryunosuke Satoro

"I learned this, at least, by my experiment: that if one advances confidently in the direction of his dreams and endeavors to live the life which he has imagined, he will meet with a success unexpected in common hours." Henry David Thoreau

"A dream you dream alone is only a dream. A dream you dream together is reality." Yoko Ono

"Champions aren't made in gyms. Champions are made from something they have deep inside them - a desire, a dream, a vision. They have to have the skill and the will. But the will must be stronger than the skill." Muhammad Ali

So what is your "Big Dream?"

Write it down here and now. Even if you haven't scripted it out fully in your mind, what would be amazing but achievable for you? What would turn you into a BADASS? Think one year out. Then think five years out. Let your mind run rampant. You can always rein it back in but you might find that you don't want to.

In The Globe and Mail (April 6, 2015), John Doyle wrote that, "a central myth of the American culture is that every American is entitled to the near religious experience of rebirth and transcendence of the shackles of the past. All of it is rooted in the origins of the United States – the European dream of redemption in the virgin land of America." As someone who left his native South Africa to reinvent himself in Canada, I am living the myth. And that's why I love motivational literature. Every story of someone else's transcendence is another deposit on my own. So share yours with me at **mike.lipkin@environics.ca**

I SHARE MY DREAM

Yesterday's notion of power was ownership. Today's notion of power is transference. Yesterday's idea of success was control. Today's idea of success is freedom. Yesterday's symbol of wealth was money. Today's symbol of wealth is influence. Yesterday's hero was self-reliant. Today's hero is ecosystemic. Yesterday's ambition was vertical. Today's ambition is forward. Yesterday was about hunting and gathering. Today is about creating and expanding.

Yesterday you may have been reticent to share your dream. Rules got in the way, layers obstructed your vision, hierarchies inhibited your mobility and beliefs blocked your momentum. Today disruptors rule. Rebels have a cause. Status quo isn't sustainable. Impossible is obsolete. Inventing is the new fixing. The dream is just a 3D print away.

Every business I'm working with is being revolutionized. The industrial age has become the internet age. It's not the service economy or the sharing economy or the experience economy. It's the dream economy. The present is indistinguishable from the future. Amazing is the new satisfactory. Continuous dreaming may be the most practical thing you can do.

We're all competing against the fantasy.

We're evaluating ourselves against the hyper-efficiency of Amazon, the virtual humanity of Apple or the ultra-consistency of Starbucks. Delight has been formularized and turned into science. Perfect is being achieved every day and compared to perfect, it's excruciatingly difficult for mere individuals to be extraordinary.

Like you, I'm continually blown away by the genius of technology and the capacity to mass-customize products that wow me. I love having my wants satisfied at the touch of a button. I'm addicted to incredible. But it's a synthetic incredible. It's an incredible that is cloned, shined and polished. It's become so omnipresent that I'm surprised when I don't get it. It's become an expected thrill.

In the presence of such magic, it's easy to minimize the magnitude of our own dream. It's easy to be overawed by the ongoing pyrotechnics around us. But here's the startling paradox: it's people and their dreams that surprise us most. The ones with stars in their eyes are the ones who help us see what's possible. Every day, they're the ones who reaffirm our belief in ourselves. They make the moment matter. They may have different styles and different skills, but they're always all in. Their enthusiasm and energy leave us feeling enthusiastic and energetic. Their excitement about what can be done makes us want to do more.

The quality of our lives is a direct function of how many people share their dreams with us. We become the company that we keep.

As the Italian writer, director and engineer, Luciano De Crescenzo, said, "we are all angels with one wing. We can only fly while embracing each other."

Share your dreams if you want to them become real. Talk about them as often as you can with whomever you can. Don't be bashful. Three things will happen:

First, you'll gain greater clarity. Things sound very different inside your own head. You don't really know what you think until you hear yourself share your thoughts with others. Unless you give them a chance to come out, they just get tangled up inside.

Second, you will receive feedback that expands the scope of your dream. Others have insights that you could never see simply because you're only looking at the prize through your own eyes. One of the greatest compliments others can pay us is to share their dreams with us. It means they trust us with something both fragile and precious. We always want to reciprocate with ways to help them realize their dream or provide names of people who can help them develop it further. And even if we're skeptical, we provide perspective that can be valuable.

Third, words are like dandelions. They're airborne seeds. They reproduce results in the most unpredictable places. You never know where a conversation will take you. But you do know that great conversations will lead somewhere great. In today's climate, it's called a "pivot" – a shift in stance and strategy that accelerates our progress. So when you share your dreams, be open to unexpected opinions.

Even criticism can serve your purpose. Negative commentary tests your resolve. Naysayers are simply there to strengthen your backbone and motivate you to talk to even more people. J.K

Rowling was famously rejected by 12 publishers before Harry Potter and The Philosopher's Stone was accepted by Bloomsbury - and even then only at the insistence of the chairman's 8-year-old daughter. Carrie, by Stephen King, was rejected 30 times before it was published. Steve Jobs was fired from his own company. The great writer James Lee Burke said, "Every rejection is incremental payment on your dues that in some way will be translated back into your work."

Dreams are the bricks and mortar of the new age.
There has never been a better time to do what you dream. Great companies and people talk in terms of dreams. They're unabashedly naïve in their expectations. They can change their industries because they don't believe it cannot be done. They're not defending history. They're developing the future. They talk in symbols. They are secular evangelists. They want to convert you to their product or service because they believe it's the right thing for you *and* it's the right thing for them. Their dialogue is dynamic. They're even creating their own language. Hey, I may even be describing you or your company.

Everything begins with language. Without words, we cannot make sense of anything. Until we define something meaningfully, we can't see it clearly. If we don't know what it can do, we don't know how to value it. Everything is open to interpretation. Content is conceptual. The description is decisive.

Right now I'm using the vocabulary of dreams with you. I'm using words as triggers to stimulate your visions of victory and fulfilment. I'm intentionally using words that energize you and get your pulse racing. I hope you're feeling charged up and ready to spread the magic.

I'm acutely aware of my verbal impact on others. I'm also aware of their verbal impact on me. I'm always delighted with encouraging words and compliments. I'm constantly surprised by how deeply bruised I am by negative or abusive language. In fact, the older I get, the more it hurts. It goes deeper. It's harder to shrug off. I may be wiser but I'm also thinner skinned.

What's your signature vocabulary? How do others feel about themselves after talking with you? Are your words animated, enthusiastic, dynamic, optimistic, affirming, joyful, spirited, empathetic and (add your words here)? Or are they dull, grey, tired, fearful, pessimistic, complaining or just plain flat?

I have never met a champion who was also a complainer. It's impossible to share a dream in language that's anything but stellar. As you share your dream, you motivate others to share theirs. That's how dreams become true – not when they actually materialize, but when others believe in them. Dreams become true when we share them. The dream precedes the deed. First, people must see it in their minds. Then everyone will see it in reality.

Every day on my way home from my office in downtown Toronto, I walk past a Ferrari showroom. I once sat in one. I luxuriated in its perfection. I still pause to look at them every day because they're real but they're dreamlike. They're so close I can literally touch them but they also belong to a distant automotive galaxy. I don't have to own one. That's someone else's dream. I am simply moved by them to drive my dream. They're proof that dreams can be manufactured both in the factory and in the imagination.

MY DREAM IS ATTACHED TO A DEADLINE

> **"The show doesn't go on because it's ready. It goes on because it's 11:30pm on Saturday Night."**
> Lorne Michaels, Executive Producer SNL

The difference between people who live their dreams and those who spend their lives dreaming is a sense of urgency. Until something has a deadline, it doesn't animate us into action. It's simply an ethereal desire that evaporates in the heat of more pressing issues. For 40 years, Saturday Night Live has happened on Saturday nights because that's the deal. Everyone engaged in producing SNL from the producers to the writers to the performers understands that each week the dream has a deadline. It's called "going live." The imperfections, flubs and bloopers are all part of the show. Often, they make the show.

A deadline is defined as the latest time by which a task must be completed. But until you put a price on being late, the deadline will be extended indefinitely. It's the consequence of incompletion that galvanizes us into action. No consequence, no action.

This book is the realization of my dream. It's my project. There was no client or stakeholder holding my feet to the fire. Yet there were many projects that I had to complete during the writing of this book. For the past two years, my life has been a contest of deadlines. My dream is the most important thing in the world to me. But I have a living to make. I have people to satisfy. I have obligations that need to be met. I have contributions I need to make. On many occasions, I shelved my dream to do the things that needed to be done now. Over time, it became an excuse not to write. Writing is damn hard. I love to do it but at the same time I'm scared of it. Every writing session is an excruciating mental exercise. Nothing is more frightening than a blank screen and nothing is as thrilling as a screen filled with worthwhile words.

It always starts off slowly. The words are reluctant to emerge. They need to be coaxed and cajoled out of me. It's like there are multiple Mike Lipkins at work. There's the Mike who wants to write; the Mike who wants to quit; the Mike who wants to party; the Mike who doesn't believe it can be done; the Mike who feels like a champ; the Mike who feels like a chump and the Mike who somehow brings all the other Mikes together to win. That's the Mike I'm depending on to write these words. I know this story sounds familiar because I talk to so many people who wrestle with all their different selves. The "self" who wins determines the nature of the end result – everything, something or nothing.

Over time, we either honour our dreams by sacrificing the ordinary things. Or we become ordinary by sacrificing our dreams. It's okay to be ordinary, commonplace, standard, commoditized or bland. But it's not great. You can settle for ordinary and still have a good life. Just living in the USA or Canada is beyond ordinary.

The opposite of champion is mediocre. It means being okay with being just okay. Being a champion demands that we live our dreams. It means we're willing to pay the price of living our dreams because we're not willing to pay the price of *not* living our dreams. Couldda, wouldda, shouldda is the language of also-rans. And so is someday, one day or any day now. Champions impose their conditions on the world; also-rans accept the conditions the world imposes on them.

So let's go back to the meaning of deadline. The original meaning of the word, circa 1865, is a boundary around a military prison beyond which a prisoner could not venture without risk of being shot by the guards. By this definition, going past the deadline could literally be fatal. Today, we apply this lethal sentence to ourselves if we wander past our own deadlines too often. It may even be worse than 150 years ago because it's gradual. It's suicide by installment.

There is a time to forgive ourselves and move on. And then there's a time to hold ourselves strictly accountable. I've learned that everything takes longer, costs more and works differently to what we expect. Champions take on more than they should. Missing a deadline is inevitable, but it's never acceptable. The moment it happens, Champions recover remarkably and find a way to recommit to themselves.

The real moment of truth is the moment just before we go to bed at night. That's when we look at the face in the mirror and see a champion who makes good on their promise to us or we see a compromiser who underdelivers on their promise to us. It's easier to sleep with someone who keeps their promises. Who are you sleeping with?

Let's make your deadline real. Set it now. Complete this sentence: I will realize my dream by dd/mm/yyyy.

Until you write down a date and share it with someone, your dream will always be subservient to the daily crisis or emergency. I set my deadline for the completion of this book at April 30, 2016. That date became non-negotiable for me. I put other people's deadlines on hold. I let them know why. They even cheered me on. Share your deadline with me and I will do the same for you.

There will always be a minority of people who begrudge you your dreams. I call them the haters. Then there will always be a minority of people who become champions of your dream. In between is the indifferent majority. They're too involved with their own issues to be concerned with yours. They won't stand in your way but they won't propel you forward either. The moral of the story is to avoid the haters, seek the champions and the rest will follow. As the Greek philosopher Epictetus said, "the key is to only keep company with people who uplift you, whose presence calls forth your best."

MY DREAM STRETCHES ME TO DO MORE

Robert Browning wrote, "Ah, but a man's reach should exceed his grasp, Or what's a heaven for?"

There are many definitions of heaven but the one I like the most is, "A condition or place of great happiness, delight or pleasure." That's the place I want to enter while I'm alive. I also know that entrance isn't free. The right of admission is reserved for those people who have made the stretch. The stretch is what makes it heaven.

Hell is a heaven that is too easily entered. Happiness is a direct function of the problems you've overcome to achieve it. Pleasure means nothing without pain, and winning means nothing without competition. What delights us today depresses us tomorrow without new, improved or different. Just try watching the same movie over and over again.

There are three kinds of happy.

There is the happiness that comes from being content, relaxed or entertained. I'm truly happy when I'm immersed in beauty on a Greek Island, eating, drinking and partying with my favourite people. This is called "hedonic happiness." It's the happiness of consumption. The environment and the activity give me pleasure.

Second is the happiness that comes from being grateful for good fortune – love, peace, health and wealth. I'm truly happy when I focus on my family and friends, the Canada I chose to make my home and native land or my personal fitness and financial wellbeing. This is called "visceral happiness." I create an environment internally that gives me joy.

Third is the happiness that comes from expanding our capacity to achieve remarkable results. I'm truly happy when I develop new content that wows people into action. Or when I win a new client or deliver a preeminent presentation. This is called "earned happiness." I have to make a contribution that others find uniquely valuable.

Hedonic, visceral and earned happiness are intertwined. All work and no play is a recipe for fatigue and burnout. The inability to experience gratitude on demand will corrode you from the inside out. And not achieving self-actualization that is appreciated by others will stymie your ability to afford hedonic happiness.

Your dream introduces the positive tension that pulls all the forms of happiness together. It stimulates you to go further when you want to give up. It sustains you when you're spent. It inspires you when you're tempted to be pessimistic. When you cannot see something in reality, you must be able to see it in your own mind.

The opposite of tension is slack. It's a sign that something or someone is being underutilized. Over time, that's how things shrink. It's called entropy – the gradual process of degradation that reduces something to nothing. On the other hand, healthy systems and people are fully employed. They're consistently evolving to take on bigger challenges and confront greater resistance. The goal is not to reduce the tension in one's life. The goal is to increase it in the right kind of way. That's your dream.

Dreams are like gravity for the mind.

According to NASA, gravity is not just a force it's also a signal – a signal telling the body how to act. It tells muscles and bones how strong they must be. In zero G, muscles atrophy quickly because the body perceives it does not need them. The muscles used to fight gravity like those in the calves and spine, which maintain posture, can lose around 20 percent of their mass if you don't use them. Muscle mass can vanish at a rate as high as five percent a week. For bones the loss can be even more extreme. Models suggest the total loss could reach 40 to 60 percent.

Blood feels gravity, too. Within two to three days of weightlessness, astronauts can lose as much as 22 percent of their blood volume. This change affects also the heart. "If you have less blood," explains Dr. Victor Schneider, research medical officer for NASA headquarters, "then your heart doesn't need to pump as hard. It's going to atrophy."

Most space adaptations appear to be reversible, but the rebuilding process is not necessarily easy. And bone recovery has proven problematic. For a three to six month space flight, Schneider says, it might require two to three years to regain lost bone, if it's going to come back and some studies have suggested that it doesn't. "You really have to exercise a lot," Schneider says. "You really have to work at it."

Dreams are like gravity for the mind. They're a signal telling the mind how to act. Without dream-tension, the mental muscle weakens and the heart grows smaller. Stress is good when it's attached to the prize. Pressure propels us forward. Our capacity expands or contracts in direct proportion to the challenges we set it.

In his play, Twelfth Night, Shakespeare said, "Be not afraid of greatness. Some are born great, some achieve greatness and others have greatness thrust upon them." Like grandmaster chess prodigy, Garry Kasparov who in 1985 became the youngest undisputed World Chess Champion at age 22, you may be born great. Or like Sully Sullenberg, the airplane pilot who was forced to land his plane in the Hudson River, you may have greatness thrust upon you. Or like 99.9 percent of people, you may have to achieve greatness. **Greatness is the state you experience when you achieve your dream.** Don't be afraid of it. It's the difference between a life of chronic desperation and joyous celebration. Dreams and desperation are mutually exclusive. We can be desperate to survive but we are always hungry for our dreams. That's why champions eat very well.

MY DREAM UPLIFTS OTHERS TO ACHIEVE THEIR DREAM

A selfish dream is like a fat turkey – it will never fly. Your dream must enable others' dreams otherwise it will never get off the ground. The secret sauce is other people's excitement about making your dream happen.

Champions know they have to sell their dreams to the people who will benefit from them. The bigger the dream, the harder the sell. There's a direct correlation between the scale of your vision and the effort required to captivate your community. Great opportunities come with great problems.

Sam Mizrahi

Sam Mizrahi is the ultimate dream merchant. Mizrahi is a 43-year-old Iranian immigrant who has built a highly successful property development company in Toronto. In addition to a collection of boutique homes and condominiums, Mizrahi is developing "Toronto's most coveted piece of real estate" (Toronto Life, February 24, 2015) at One Bloor Street West. Mizrahi is planning the second highest building in Canada; an 80-storey skyscraper designed by the famed British architect Norman Foster.

There were many developers who wanted to get their hands on the site. In his own words, here's how Mizrahi prevailed.

> "The process took close to 11 months. The one thing that I did differently was to understand what the property owners felt and wanted, besides the financial aspect of the transaction.

When you have people who have owned the property for 114 years, it becomes a very emotional decision. It's not just the numbers. It's a matter of sharing the same value system. You have to have a great deal of empathy.

I met with them constantly. We'd talk about the past, the present and the future. And sometimes we'd talk about nothing related to the property. We'd just talk about life in general. It became a trusted friendship and you can't fake that. So we were able to mutually sit down as friends and figure it out together.

Simplicity was very important to Ed Whaley (an owner). In the old world, things were simple. It was about handshakes. I subscribed to that value system and Ed knew that. It's about doing what you say and fulfilling your promises. I gained a friend out of it. It wasn't just a transaction.

I met with architects in New York, London, France and Canada and we looked at many different ways we could develop this corner in a way that would put Toronto on the international architecture stage. It's a matter of fitting a new building in the context of what is being built around it and what is going to be built. Retail is the most significant component of this development. This is the nexus of the retail core in Toronto, if not Canada. We wanted PATH (underground pedestrian) connections and TTC (subway) connections. And the new retail format asks for uncontaminated space, which means you don't have columns or pillars running through it. The residential aspect is going to be unlike anything that Toronto has seen.

I applaud what's happening in Toronto. I trumpet what's happening in Toronto. I think we're very blessed and we have to be very grateful for how Toronto is transforming and maturing into an international city. We're a mosaic of cultures. We're like the UN. We're very diverse with very sophisticated palates. I think the growth we're seeing and the number of cranes that are up, is a testament to how successful Toronto has been.

I'm somewhat of a micromanager. I get very passionate about the details. I'm involved in everything, right down to the colour of the mortar that goes in the brick, right down to the caulking colour, right down to the details of the hinges on the doors. I've found that very few buildings have soul to them and we want to bring that to Yonge and Bloor.

What you're going to see is an iconic structure that will be 80-storeys tall. You're going to see an exoskeletal building. There will be jewellery on the building that creates an artistic weave. You're going to have something that's never been done before in Toronto or Canada, for that matter.

We're not interested in creating something that is not tasteful or that's not timeless. Ego is one of those things you hang at the door."

That's how to sell the dream – right down to the hinges of the doors. For Sam Mizrahi, the dream is building an 80-storey skyscraper that elevates Toronto's evolution into an international city. For Mike Lipkin the dream is creating a blueprint that turns people into champions while they champion others. What's it for you? How can you sell your dream in a way that inspires people to make it happen with you?

You may be a natural extrovert. Or you may be innate introvert. It doesn't matter. You need to do whatever's necessary to bring your dream to life. It may be easier if you're a P.T. Barnum kind of person, but I've discovered the most effective pitch-people are more reserved. They don't come across as too slick or too rehearsed. Their credibility is higher because their authenticity and humanity shines through. As you seek to uplift others, your dream uplifts you.

As a professional speaker, I'm often asked how I handle the nervousness that precedes a keynote talk. The truth is I still get nervous before every presentation. There's always a moment of terror as you contemplate the consequences of failure. The temptation is too great not to think what could go wrong. I've learned to endure those flashes of fear and consciously focus on the impact I'm about to make on the audience. After 23 years as a motivational speaker, every engagement is another extension of my dream. I get to do what I love and what I can be the best in the world at. I remind myself of the magic. I declare my readiness to myself and I step out onto the stage. My mantra is literally: my dream uplifts others. I chant it and start talking. That's how I earn a nine-out-of-10 rating nine-times-out-of-10. I want to be conscious of myself but not self-conscious. The only thing that matters is the impact on the audience.

Don't worry about being an extrovert or an introvert. Be an "ambivert." An ambivert is someone who is whatever they need to be in every situation. Reticence can never be allowed to get in the way of your dream. On the other hand, there is a time to think, listen and be quiet. The guiding principle is: be as big as your dream or as useful as other's dreams need you to be.

The five possibility questions.

When I started talking with Michael Adams and the Environics team about starting our joint venture in 2000, Michael asked me a simple question: "How can we help you?" It's the one question that reaffirmed my decision to align with Environics. Everyone else I spoke with was only concerned about how I could contribute to their prosperity. So when you share your dream with others ask them, **"How can I help you achieve your dream?"**

Like Sam Mizrahi, make sure you know what's important to others when you're selling your dream.

Here are the four other possibility questions that should be part of any dream-dialogue:

2. What's your dream when it comes to ______?

Most people will not be able to answer this question clearly simply because they haven't been asked it before. Your role is to draw out and clarify their response. If I want people to work with me to sell 100,000 copies of this book, I need to know how doing so will champion their dream.

3. What's the most important thing for you in terms of_____?

When you help people identify their priorities, they associate you as a champion who can help them achieve their priorities. Your dream must be a conduit to their priorities.

4. What do you enjoy the most in connection with_________?

People are drawn towards pleasure and away from pain. Your dream must help them achieve both objectives.

5. Who are the people who can help us achieve the dream?

Identify the dream team and the roles for each member to play. Everyone may have different ideas about who can play a role. Make sure you've identified all the potential all-stars.

Powerful Presence comes with dreaming like a champion.

Let's pause here for a moment. Take stock of your state. Are you inspired? Are you ready to make your dream happen? Are you ready to help others make their dreams happen? I hope this book is bringing you closer to your dream. I hope you can almost touch it.

Presence is defined as actually occurring or existing in reality. When you dream like a champion, you actually come into contact with your dream. You step into your future right now. In that state, you have the power to move others. You become the bridge to their desired future. Your presence gives others permission to believe in themselves. That's the most powerful presence.

The enemy of dreams is doubt. Doubt is lack of certainty and the absence of conviction. It's the normal state for most of us almost all of the time. Violent change magnifies our doubt. We're constantly teetering on the brink of a decision: should I or shouldn't I? Sometimes the data doubles the doubt. All the information in the world may not be able to help us if we don't have the conviction to deal with it.

My most successful moments are when I'm consciously living the dream – wherever I am. I could be performing on stage. I could be engaging in a one-on-one conversation. I could be writing down my thoughts like I am now. I could be resolving a crisis or solving a problem. I could be reading a magazine or listening to a podcast. By consciously living the dream, I'm freeing the best part of me to play at my best while I help others do the same. The sweetest words I can ever hear, in my professional life are, "I needed to hear that. You helped me decide what to do."

The shining trait of champions is their capacity to remove all doubt because of their certainty and conviction. That's the ultimate thrill. When we have no doubt that we will succeed, we lose all fear of failure. We focus only on the upside. We step into the arena and take on anything that comes at us.

Think about the last dangerous thing you did where there was almost no possibility of getting hurt because you believed in the power of champions to protect you. That's why people jump out of airplanes or bungee jump, get into underwater cages and go nose-to-nose with a great white shark or climb sheer rock faces or simply go on rollercoasters. They have no doubt about the outcome.

Champions have no doubt about the outcome even when the outcome is in doubt.

They know they will win, even when they lose. As the great Vince Lombardi once said, "I never lost a game. Sometimes I just ran out of time." Life is a numbers game. A "loss" doesn't mean losing. It's simply part of winning.

By now, I have no doubt that you identify as a champion. I know that you dream like a champion. Now let's go plan like a champion.

Others can guide you, but only you can give your true power to yourself. No one else has your answers.

Once upon a time, in a land far away, there was a wealthy merchant who lived in a small village near the sea. He was a wise and prudent man who knew that he must give back to his community in thanks for what the community had given to him. So he established an extraordinary custom. Every year, he invited the poor from the village to sit at his table for an annual feast. He lavished copious amounts of food and drink on his amazed and hungry guests. Part of the annual ritual, however, was the announcement that he always made at the end of the day's merriment.

> "Take everything. Take whatever you want. Take it home with you."

The wealthy merchant would then watch as his guests helped themselves to his entire household - the furniture, the clothes, the crockery and the cutlery, his horses, even the lanterns on his gates - anything that they could remove and carry away.

On this one particular occasion, a poor peasant watched the merchant closely throughout the day. He noticed that every time the merchant rang a glass bell that he kept close to him, servants rushed in with heaps of food and drink. The peasant waited for the end of the meal when the usual announcement was made. Immediately, he asked the merchant:

> "May I have the bell?"

Slightly amused, the merchant handed the peasant the bell. The peasant ran home with the bell. He told his wife to lay the table and invite all their neighbours and friends. When all was ready, he sat down at the table and rang the bell. Nothing happened. He rang it again and again. He rang it until it shattered. He felt a deep sense of despair. He felt he had been cheated.

Does this ring a bell with you? Have you ever sought the advice or insight of another person, only to find that it didn't work for you?

Worse still, have you ever been disappointed or lost money because someone else's strategy was totally inappropriate for you? How many times you have attended a seminar or course where you felt excited and empowered, only to have the inspiration desert you the very next day? A lot of the time, right?

Here's the essence of this "life principle": No one else has your answers. At most, they can guide you, they can counsel you, they can illuminate your path, but they cannot act for you. That you must do. And it all begins with a plan.

3

PLAN LIKE A CHAMPION

UNDERSTAND YOUR ENVIRONMENT: CONTEXT IS EVERYTHING

BUILD A WINNING MINDSET: BE A “CERTAINIST”

BUILD THE YIN AND YANG OF YOUR “PERSONAL BRAND PLAN”

A PLAN IS ONLY AS GOOD AS THE PEOPLE YOU ENROL IN THE PLAN

AS THINGS CHANGE, CHANGE YOUR PLAN

PLAN LIKE A CHAMPION

> **"Every operation in the military is based on a five paragraph order and the acronym is SMEAC – situation, mission, execution, administration, and communication. It's a very logical flow."**
> Don Knauss, CEO The Clorox Company

"Plan" is a verb as well as a noun. As a verb, it means to design a course of action with a specific future in mind. As a noun, it means a method or process created to achieve a specific result. It also means a drawing made to scale to represent the top view or a horizontal section of a structure or a machine, as in a floor layout of a building.

The point of planning is to create the method or process that leads us where we want to go. It delivers direction and discipline. It's like a rudder steering us through unchartered waters. Planning is the antidote to panic in turbulent times. You shouldn't wait until there's a crisis to have a crisis plan. Yet until there is a crisis, there may be no urgency to create a plan. The secret is to create an inner urgency to form a plan.

One thing is certain, you will be confronted with a monumental crisis when you least expect it or when it's most inconvenient. We're never exactly ready for a crisis, but a plan accelerates our readiness. It imbues us with confidence so we can preempt the ultimate disabler – self-doubt. Champions live by the mantra, "Often wrong, but never in doubt." The difference between wrong and right can be marginal. Wrong can become right in a heartbeat if you stay on plan.

The opposite of a crisis is a breakthrough. But it's often the crisis that generates the breakthrough, especially if you take action. As Rahm Emanuel, the mayor of Chicago, says, "a crisis is a terrible thing to waste." And so is luck. Luck is a breakthrough without the crisis. It's a gift that comes with a condition: immediate, appropriate action. Even when opportunity is served to you on a platter, you still have to take it. Without a plan, it's easy to miss it.

After 23 years of coaching and motivating people around the world, I've discovered that success is not a result of luck. Luck by itself is a fluke. It's a one-off event that isn't likely to be repeated. There is no such thing as consistent luck unless you have a plan. That's called ROL – "Return on Luck." It's earned results sustained by constant commitment to your plan.

We may not be able to see around corners, but we can sense things. Planning sharpens our acuity – our ability to discern details invisible to others. A detective sees clues in the chaos. A geologist sees gold through the rock. A doctor detects the disease beneath the skin. And a champion wins the contest long before the contest.

This book is a cornerstone of my plan. I'm writing these words on New Year's Day 2016. It must be complete by the end of April. I'm introducing the urgency required to complete it because without urgency, nothing gets completed. I also know that without it, I won't have something fresh and enticing to share with my clients in 2016. That will be bad for business and tragic for me. That's a worst-case scenario that haunts me – being a speaker with nothing new to say. By writing these words now, I'm planning a spectacular new business year that begins in a few months.

So what's your plan? How are you designing a future you want live into? If you don't design your own future, someone else will design it for you and they may not have your best interests in mind. Either way, it's a scary thing to do. When you design your own future, you're consciously channeling yourself in a tightly defined direction. You're eliminating all the alternatives that fall outside the range of your process. On the other hand, if you let your environment and other people design your future, you slide towards a destination by default.

Operating without a plan is frustration waiting to happen. Minutes turn into hours, hours turn into days, days turn into months and months turn into years. There's no such thing as making up for lost time. There's just the numbing sense of potential that went to seed. The future is a function of what we do right now. So what are you doing to design your future?

Whatever you do, you're certain to end up somewhere. If you don't know where you're going, every road is an option. Too many options will make you insane, angry, upset or disillusioned. Whenever I counsel someone in the throes of career or life indecision, it's usually because they don't have a design or model to evaluate their decisions against. They feel uneasy and adrift because they're being borne along a current that they didn't cause.

According to a 2014 Oxfam Report, the top one percent of people control half the wealth in the world. The bottom 80 percent have to make do with 5.5 percent leaving 19 percent to get by with the rest.

After 23 years of working with champions, I have discovered that one percent of people have a clearly defined plan for their life. There's a remarkable correlation between those who control wealth and those who plan to control wealth. We become what we plan to be.

I often hear people state ruefully, "I never planned for this to happen." The real problem is that they didn't plan for anything to happen. They just went along to get along.

T.S. Eliot

T.S. Eliot wrote, "When forced to work within a strict framework the imagination is taxed to its utmost – and will produce its richest ideas. Given total freedom the work is likely to sprawl." Our plan and the act of planning formulate the framework that focuses our foresight.

We all need some kind of blinkers that keep our eyes on the prize. The alternative is a chronic state of attention deficit that cripples our personal power. Listen in stereo, but see in "monovision." That's where the money is. That's where the plan will take you.

The great writer Albert Camus commented, "Life is a sum of all your choices." Every day we will make multiple choices when faced with multiple alternatives. Most of the time the choices will be automatic and routinized. We will be guided by our past, our culture, our conscience or our habits. But every day, we are confronted with inflection points that can change our trajectory if we're aware of them and we respond accordingly.

For example, I can choose to work out today or not. I can choose to attend a community meeting today or not. I can choose to write or not. I can choose to read today or not. I can choose to spend time with my children today or not. I can choose to give time and money or not. I can choose to eat fruit and vegetables today or not. I can choose to invest in stocks today or not. I can choose to reach out to friends or not. Today I can choose to research business opportunities or not. Each one of these actions is a choice. And each choice is part of my plan or not. Every day a little becomes a lot.

I'm making all these choices real time but the plan enables me to be spontaneous. I'm running on a mind-ware program that guides my behaviour in a conscious direction. There are many moments when I would not have acted in a desirable way if I didn't follow the plan I'm about to share with you.

I call it the "serious pursuit of serendipity." Serendipity is the faculty for making desirable discoveries by accident. It's when we collide with luck to get what we want. But when you're following a plan, you have more happy collisions. By engaging in each of the conscious behaviours that I outlined, I multiply my chances of success. Victory goes to those who are most often in the right place at the right time with the right people.

The three questions we're all asking ourselves all the time are: What's really going on around me? What's really going to happen next? What should I really do now?

Whether you're aware of it or not, our research shows you've been asking yourself variations on three questions while you've been reading this book:

First you're asking: what's really going on around me? What's shaping my reality? What should I be paying attention to? What and who could hurt me? What and who could help me? What are the real drivers? What am I not seeing that I should be seeing? Am I even facing the right direction?

We all have a nagging sense that things are not what they seem. We've been surprised so many times we're not even surprised anymore when we're surprised. Still it always jars us. We never become inured to shock or pain.

Second you're asking: what's really going to happen next? Where are things headed? How are things changing? What will the outcome be? How can I anticipate the future so I'm not blindsided by it? What are the patterns and where are they leading?

We all want to know what's going to happen so we can place our bets accordingly. Lightning can strike us if we're in the right place. We want to create our own luck. We know there are people who know more than us and we want to talk to them. As mere mortals, we only have five senses but we want the Spidey-sense that warns us when something is about to happen.

Third you are asking: what should I really do now? How should I be preparing and protecting myself? How can I succeed? Who should I be partnering with? How can I become most valuable to the people who are most valuable to me? What am I not doing that I'm going to pay for later?

Peace of mind comes with knowing you're doing all you can with all you have. That's the plan. That's how you convert the unknown into the raw material for the achievement of your dreams.

No one else knows what is right for you. No one can get inside your head and write your plan for you. But they can *guide* you to create the plan that's right for you. That's what I'm doing right now. The template I'm about to share is proven and powerful. It's the culmination of all my research and personal experience. It's helped me achieve a level of success that still amazes me every day. And I know it can do the same for you.

The perfect place to be is where you don't want to be anywhere else.

When I ask people to describe their perfect place, they usually describe a physical location that makes them happy. It may be up in the mountains or down by the sea. It may be their favourite restaurant or their favourite city. It could be where they vacation or where they hang with their friends.

The truth is that the perfect place is a space we create for ourselves independent of circumstances. I've been miserable in the Mediterranean in May and euphoric in Des Moines in December. We take ourselves wherever we go. Sometimes external beauty can weigh us down because it contradicts our internal states. What's more, external beauty alone has a short shelf life. Paradise without work to come back to is purgatory.

So think about the perfect place inside you. It's when you feel like you're both at home and away. You feel content and challenged. You're satisfied and stretched. You can relax but you're alert and tuned in at the same time. That's the place where you aren't thinking about being anywhere else with anyone else. You know you're where you're supposed to be because that's where you are.

This is the place where you defy age. You radiate conviction. You conjure up your best thoughts and you follow through with bold actions. You become new again because that's who you're always being. You're the kind of person who is a tonic and elixir to others.

People who know you also know they can always rely on you to energize and educate them. People who meet you for the first time are instantly aware of your joie de vivre and vitality. You may be loud or you may be muted. Your style doesn't matter because you're in a place where your light will always shine through.

I know I've just described a rare place of power. But this book is all about people who live there. You may be closer to that place than you think. In fact, you're already spending time there. Now you need to explore how to be there more often. Think of people you know who live there most of the time. The more time you spend with them, the more time you will spend in your perfect place. Then you will pay it forward.

The truth is that our perfect place is a balance between scarcity and abundance. We need scarcity to stimulate our creative juices. Scarcity drives us to ask new questions and find new answers. Scarcity breeds urgency and urgency causes action. On the other hand, abundance can lead to laziness. We can afford to procrastinate and prevaricate because we aren't punished for inaction. Inefficiency isn't painful when resources are plentiful. We need to find our own threshold of effectiveness where we achieve just the right balance of tension and reflection.

Becoming new again is the oldest desire in the world. It's also a choice to be foolish.

We all age but not all of us become old. Youth is a mindset not just a chronological fact. It's a philosophy that's lived every day. I look at Mick Jagger, Jerry Seinfeld, Robert Redford, Meryl Streep, Maggie Smith, Desmond Tutu, Richard Branson or Christopher Plummer and I see people striving to do the best work of their lives. They're on fire with the possibilities. Every year is merely another deposit into their talent bank.

They've made the choice to rejuvenate themselves with every performance. The Random House dictionary defines rejuvenation as, "restore to youthful vigor; make young again." It can be done but it's more than skin deep. It goes all the way to the soul.

There's a saying that there is no fool like an old fool. If we define "fool" as an ardent enthusiast who will do anything to pursue his interest, rather than stupid, then older fools are merely more ardent enthusiasts. I'm a proud member of that fraternity. I have chosen enthusiasm over resignation, just like I've chosen fascination over fatigue.

It isn't easy but it's the only way to be. That's my core belief. It underpins everything I do – from the food I eat to the people I meet. I've made the choice to be this way and I practice my choice every day. This book is my "Declaration of Rejuvenation." I don't want to live forever. I just want to be young when I die.

Some of the oldest people I know are the youngest. The stronger their sense of mortality, the greater their appetite for life. Their only fear is they're not living life to the full. They're childlike but not childish. No matter how many years of life they have, they're still easily wowed. They experience the rush but they're not rushed. They've learned to savour each moment because they know how extraordinary each one is.

Here's what may sound like a stupid question: how many cups of coffee have you had in your lifetime? One thousand? Ten thousand? Thirty thousand? When you sip your next cup of coffee, will it be merely one of thousands you have before? Or will it be your very first cup? Will it be an entirely new experience because you've never had that specific cup of coffee before? Will you experience the same degree of wonder? Or will you utter my four most abhorred words in the English language: same old, same old? If you ever find yourself even thinking these words, replace them immediately with new again, new again.

We become new again when we're open, healthy, strong, optimistic, inspired, sponge-like, trusting and loving. I know that sounds like a personal nirvana. But it's one that we can create because it's all on the inside. It's a function of our mindset and motion. It's a commitment to joy irrespective of circumstance. It's understanding that no matter how grueling or gut-wrenching our experiences are, we always have a personal choice to make: do I become bigger or bitter? That's the difference between excitement and anger, delight or despair, generosity or stinginess.

What is your relationship to "New?"

At every stage of our lives, we begin the next cycle of "New." Sometimes we travel alone and sometimes we run with a pack. Sometimes we go down paths that are well trodden and sometimes we make new ones.

Sometimes, new is the kind of new we want and sometimes it's thrust on us. Sometimes new means pleasure, sometimes new means pain. We can act out of necessity or obligation. Or we can act out of passion for work, play, relationships and community. Sometimes, we have something to prove. And sometimes, something needs to prove itself to us.

One thing is for sure: we will all fail at some point. Maybe we hit a roadblock we can't get around. Maybe we will meet our nemesis – the person who intimidates and torments us. Maybe we'll experience an alarming or traumatic event. Maybe someone valuable to us will let us down badly. Maybe someone fresher and sharper enters the game. Maybe the game itself changes and we struggle to change with it. And maybe we'll just be worn down by the wear and tear of life.

At a time when we least expect it, we go from being the fresh, new talent to the incumbent cramming to keep up. We become the representative of the status quo. We turn into yesterday's hero and today's cautionary tale. It becomes harder and harder to be noticed. Our value declines as we earn less attention. Our rhythm becomes a routine that becomes a rut. We run as fast as we can just to stop the decline. Effortless grace becomes tough slogging.

So what do you do? Do you just hang in and hang on? Do you try to regenerate yourself as "new and improved"? Do you hope that you've laid a strong enough foundation to rise to the next level? Do you pray for someone to champion your cause or ride to your rescue? Do you jump ship? Do you change jobs? Do you change careers?

Where are you in the ageing cycle?

Are you brand new? Are you building your mastery? Are you cramming to catch up? Or are you sliding into decline?

Being new always ends abruptly. And the *next* new begins. It's called the future. We can be "the new" or we can be replaced by "the next new." Stagnation is not an option. We can go big but we can't just go home. Sometimes, we need to relax in our safe haven. We need to cocoon ourselves against the craziness of the outside world. But we can't stay there beyond a short timeout. Too much time in a shelter will make us soft. The stress of confinement becomes suffocating. We may feel safe, but we don't feel alive. If you stay at home too long, you grow old, heavy, tired and scared.

We need the systems and the structure that facilitates our functioning. But no matter how organized and efficient we are, we need to be open to change. Otherwise we end up minding a machine that's obsolete. We go stale from the inside out. Entropy, the steady deterioration of a person or society, is a horrible way to die. On the other hand, rejuvenation is an invigorating way to live.

So what's your relationship to new? Does it occur to you as a threat? Or an invitation to thrive? Or both?

THE SIX STAGES OF BEING ALWAYS NEW:

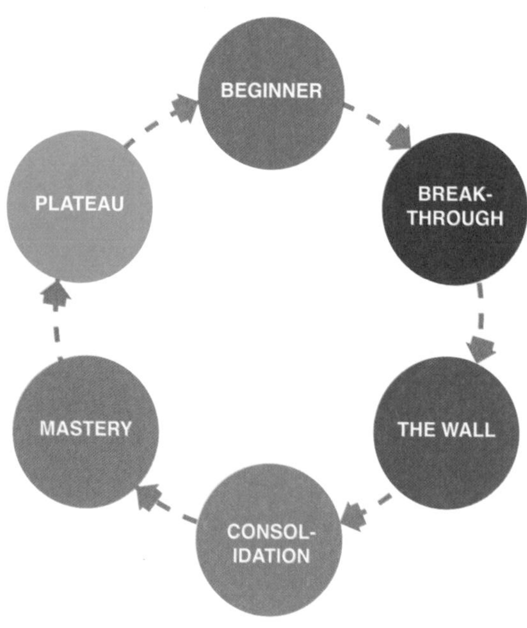

Stage One - Beginner:

Once upon a time, we were all new. We were the beginners. We were the elixir. Whatever we were, we weren't the past. We were the relief from the routine. We were in a place that we weren't before. We were noticed and recognized and celebrated.

If we were lucky enough to do what we loved, the future stretched out like a yellow brick road. Pure potential is a beautiful thing. Excitement is a powerful fuel. Not knowing it cannot be done is a lucrative space to occupy.

There is such a thing as "Beginner's Luck." It is the exponential rise in skill that accompanies early efforts. It's the joy of competing and enthusiasm that comes with the initial mastery of new disciplines. It's the application of new ideas and strategies. It is the aphrodisiac that animates our performance and magnetizes others to us. It's the nostalgic reminder to them of how they used to be when *they* were new.

Remember how that felt inside? The fascination, the curiosity, the pleasure and the fulfilment? And remember how it felt on the outside? The admiration, the recognition, the kudos, the success and the rewards? It's intoxicating. When it starts like that, it seems like it will never end.

Stage Two – Breakthrough:

Joy is a powerful fuel. When you blend it with consistently positive feedback, the octane rises even higher. The more action you take, the more momentum you build. And so does your network and skill-set. Success is a beautiful thing. You want more and you're willing to do whatever it takes to get it. The payoffs are a powerful narcotic.

You experience breakthrough after breakthrough as you grow your confidence and competence. Defeat is not an option. Pessimism is an alien emotion. It's all fresh, shiny and hot. When you're new, you don't know what it's like to be old. But when you're old, you remember what it's like to be new.

Stage Three – The Wall:

All good things come to an end. Sometimes you break barriers. And sometimes the barriers break you. What seems easy at the start becomes difficult further down the path. Ignorance can be bliss when experience can be painful. The unknown is exciting until it proves it's nothing like what we expected. What worked before doesn't work anymore. We confront situations that suddenly seem indecipherable. There is a reason why paths remain untrodden.

When we don't deliver, our champions can become nemeses. We see the dark side of the dream. Frustration exhausts us. We push harder but we go nowhere. We feel overloaded and overwhelmed. We enter a forced slowdown. Our faith wavers. We question our commitment to the course and cause.

Frustration is a persistent feeling of dissatisfaction, often accompanied by tension and anxiety. It's sourced from unfulfilled needs or unresolved problems. It's also the result of applying ineffective strategies. Frustration is corrosive because we direct our internal negativity towards others. We see them as part of the problem. Being in the presence of a frustrated person is deeply unsettling. It's a lose-lose environment because a frustrated person is like someone who is either inebriated or exhausted. They can't be reasoned with. Until they relax and let go of their dissonance, the only possible outcome is stalemate. "Just sleep on it" may be the best advice to give them.

It all ends here. Or it all starts here. The vast majority of people turn around when they hit the wall. It's too high. It's too thick. It's too wide. It's too immovable. This is where the "dabblers" are separated from the "determinators." Walls are there to keep the uncommitted ones out.

Stage Four – Consolidation:

> **"There is a tide in the affairs of men. Which, taken at the flood, leads on to fortune; Omitted, all the voyage of their life is bound in shallows and in miseries. On such a full sea are we now afloat, and we must take the current when it serves, or lose our ventures."** William Shakespeare, Julius Caesar

This is my favourite quote. It expresses the inflection point we all reach multiple times in our lives. That's when we choose to capitulate to the moment or we choose to capitalize on it. Whatever we choose, it becomes a habit. Either we take the bull by the horns or the bull takes us.

There's a reason why you hit the wall in the first place. You were carried along by your passion and talent in equal measure. You're good yet great is on the other side of the wall. You've got to want it bad enough. But you also need the presence of mind to step back before you step back in.

There's a theme that runs through every story of great success. It's the stumble, fumble and fall after an unbroken streak of wins. It's when the hero or heroine needs to fundamentally reexamine their mission. They need to review their approach. They need to reset their strategy. They need to reengage their world and everything in it. It's a time of heartache and soul-searching. But it's also the gateway to the next level.

Stage Five – Mastery:

There is a secret to everything. A secret is defined as "a method, formula or plan known only to the initiated or the few." If you've got the will and you do the work, your calling gives up its secret to you. You crack the code of great. You discover the essence of excellence.

Your understanding unleashes a whole new level of effectiveness. Every action yields a higher return. You hit your sweet spot. You see things that you never saw before. You play from reflex while you enhance your game at the same time. Everything appears brighter and clearer. You go faster, deeper, longer.

And the word gets out. People talk about your prowess. Your achievements garner acclaim. You become a magnet for opportunity and talent. You spend less time on the things that don't count so you can invest more time on things that do. What used to wear you down now sharpens you up. You're recognized as a master of your craft. And that's when you enter the danger zone.

Stage Six – Plateau:

It takes effort to make it effortless. The better you become, the more you need to invest to become even better. The best performers are the hardest workers. There's no timeout for good behaviour. No matter what your field, you have to pay the price for success. And the price gets steeper as you climb higher.

The going gets tough at high altitudes. It's easy to run out of gas. Or the lack of oxygen can trick you into believing that you can just cruise to the finish line. Whatever the cause, mastery is perishable. It goes stale if it's not revitalized. Rejuvenation comes with the territory. Or, you simply make the choice to flatline into the sunset. The world is full of former maestros who decided to suspend their quest for new because it becomes just too hard, too uncomfortable and too threatening. There is an old Zen proverb that says, "If your mind is empty, it is always ready for anything, it is open to everything. In the beginner's mind there are many possibilities, but in the expert's mind there are few." So that's the ultimate paradox – achieving mastery means becoming an expert but becoming an expert means losing mastery.

The resolution is to understand that while knowledge is always valuable, expertness is a fleeting state. All your knowledge is valuable because it enables you to acquire more knowledge. If the mind is a muscle, knowledge is the training that makes it stronger. But mastery depends on embracing the new, unburdened by the past. The past becomes a platform from which to spring. It frees you up because you're willing to jettison whatever doesn't work in favour of what does. In short, you're willing to become a beginner all over again.

No matter how comfortable you might be with others or others might be with you, you need to bring "new" to the relationship if you want it to thrive. Unconditional love may exist between a man and his dog, a parent and her child or a person and their God. Otherwise, all love is earned through the continuous pursuit of new ways to bring value, especially in the workplace. So that's the plan – to be always new, especially when you're not new.

THE FIVE PARTS OF A CHAMPION'S PLAN

1. Understand your environment: context is everything
2. Build a winning mindset
3. Build the yin and yang of your "Personal Brand Plan"
4. Enrol others
5. Change with change

1. Understand your environment: context is everything

> **"I am not sure that we will still use Apple products in 25 years, but I am sure that we will still be drinking Dom Perignon. Technology is predicated on change. Luxury is predicated on heritage and connection to tradition."** Bernard Arnault, Chairman, LVMH

Once upon a time, in a desert land far away, there lived a humble man called Ahmed. Ahmed didn't have much, but what he did have were two assets that served him well: a marvellously calm temperament and a magnificent black stallion.

The stallion was not only Ahmed's pride and joy; it was also his means of making a living. For a handsome fee, neighbours from miles around would bring their mares to Ahmed to be "covered" by his stallion. Every time one of these neighbours laid eyes on

Ahmed's stallion, they would sigh with envy. "You are so lucky to have this horse," they would say to him over and over again. "Maybe and maybe not," Ahmed would reply enigmatically.

Then, one day tragedy struck. The stallion's caretaker left the stable door open and the horse disappeared. The neighbours heard of the tragedy and called Ahmed with their condolences. "This is terrible news," they said to him. "Maybe and maybe not," he replied enigmatically.

Three days later, the horse reappeared as if by magic. What's more, he brought with him two other stallions that he had befriended while wandering in the desert. The neighbours called to congratulate him. "Now you've got three stallions to hire out. You're going to be rich. You're so lucky. This is wonderful news," they cried. "Maybe and maybe not," Ahmed replied enigmatically.

Now, Ahmed had a 16-year-old son, Rachbar, whom he loved very much. Rachbar loved horses and he was a natural horseman. He saw the new stallions and immediately mounted one of them. The wild horse felt the strange, unwelcome weight on his back and threw the boy off. As Rachbar landed, he broke both legs. When the neighbours heard the news, they immediately called Ahmed to commiserate with him. "We are so sorry for you and your son," they cried, "This is terrible news." Of course, Ahmed replied, as he always did, "Maybe and maybe not."

The next week, it was announced that an adjacent state had declared war on Ahmed's country. The government, desperate for troops, conscripted all boys over the age of 15 for battle. These boys had little or no military training. Their chances of survival were slim indeed. But the government couldn't take Ahmed's son because his legs were broken. So when the government took away all the neighbours' sons for battle, they looked enviously at Ahmed and cried in unison, "You're so lucky!" And what was Ahmed's response? You guessed it.

We're often blind to change because change is too close or too far, too slow or too fast, too loud or too soft. Where we stand determines what we see and what we do.

While you read this, you're changing. Every breath determines what we're becoming. We know we're growing older but we can't see ourselves from inside our own heads. Even the face we see in the mirror isn't the face that others see. Everything is an interpretation by someone else.

Sometimes change appears to be immediate and dramatic. Sometimes it appears to be sudden. Sometimes it appears subtle. Sometimes it appears favourable and sometimes it appears fearful. Sometimes it seems like nothing is changing when everything is.

As Sam Tanenhaus wrote in The New York Times (August 17, 2014),
"In the age of the start up, of fortunes gained and lost overnight, of flawed ideas in need of continual debugging and retweaking, failure is the default outcome and also, at times, the ground zero of eventual triumph." Tanenhaus adds that according to a 2014 Pew research report, "millennials are the nation's most dogged optimists – they believe their own best days are ahead."

Success means seeing the change and being able to influence the change. Seeing the change means recognizing the pattern and projecting it into the future. There is a logic and rhythm to everything. Every change is either an extension of the pattern or a disruption of it. We need to step back enough to recognize the pattern but be close enough to see the details of it. We need to zoom out and then we need to zoom in. And we need to know when to do what.

But to see the change and not be able to influence the change is a tragedy of Cassandra-like proportions. In Greek mythology, Cassandra was the daughter of Priam, the King of Troy. Apollo, the son of Zeus and the god of music, fire and light, was captivated by her beauty. As part of his attempt to seduce her, he gave her the gift of prophecy. But when she resisted him, he placed a curse on her so that no one would believe her predictions. She was left with knowledge of the future but no power to influence it.

We are all part of the change process. Whether we're just observers or primary movers of change, our mere presence influences what happens next. Observers affect what is being observed. The size of the audience impacts the context of the performance. The great players adjust their game accordingly. They thrive in the clutch moments while their opponents choke.

In the April 2014 issue of Fast Company, Ed Catmull, CEO of Pixar, said it best, "There is no stable place. But there is this illusion that somehow you can get to a stable place, figure it all out. People have their fear: They want to be in a secure place; they want to know what to do; they want people to tell them what to do. And there isn't anything that can remove that underlying piece of human nature. It is when we try to avoid, stop or control change that we get into trouble."

There is no secure place if you define secure as "no-change." The future belongs to those who are professors of change. They are the people who understand their current circumstances so deeply they can anticipate what will happen next. They discern what's lying just beneath the surface so they can sense when it will emerge. They're always plugged in and ready to play.

Context is everything. The trends will sweep us along whether we're aware of them or not. Success without awareness is a one-time thing. The world is full of stories of people who have soared for a moment and then plummeted back to earth.

On the other hand, champions build "intentional awareness." They look very hard for what they hope to find. They're constantly studying the trends transforming their world. They're enhancing their consciousness and developing their antennae. They may not be able to see the future, but they have a good sense of where it's headed.

So pause for a moment. Think about the main trends defining your professional space. What are the major moves? Where are the signs pointing? Where is the dotted line heading?

Write down the top three trends transforming your world and their implications for your future.

THE TOP THREE TRENDS INFLUENCING YOUR WORLD

1. ______________________________
2. ______________________________
3. ______________________________

If you look carefully, you will see what you're looking for.

The message is between the minutiae. When you strip away the distractions, you can see the patterns defining your future.

In a professional sense, when we listen to others, we're really listening for assurance that they know what they're talking about. Our trust is a direct function of our belief in others' understanding of what will happen next. Clearly articulated knowledge is power.

You're reading this book as a way to increase your "intentional awareness." I'm enabling you to think about the key factors that could shape your future. Anything is obvious once it's been thought of. The challenge is to constantly allocate the time and energy to understand your environment. If all you do is keep your nose close to the grindstone, you'll end up with a very short nose. So keep your head up and keep your head down in equal measure.

There is no shortcut to understanding your environment. You need to read the publications or sites that signal the key developments. You need to watch and listen to the sources that tell it like it is. You need to talk to the people who are in the know. Most importantly, you need to make it a daily discipline. Even the most successful people struggle with casting aside what is merely urgent so they can focus on what is important.

As a rule you should invest at least 20 percent of your time understanding your environment. Champions invest north of 30 percent. They are ruthless in saying no to things that get in the way of their intentional awareness. It also helps that they love to learn. They put in the hours because it isn't work for them; it's a joy. Curiosity encourages them to uncover clues that are concealed from others.

Here are ten patterns defining the future that I've uncovered through my sleuthing. I guarantee that each one is impacting your life deeply. After you've reviewed them, share your reactions with me, as well as any other patterns you've identified. The most successful forecasters are dialoguers. They operate in teams and networks. They test their hypotheses by sharing them and being open to the feedback that they receive.

Let's begin the dialogue now – email me at **mike.lipkin@environics.ca**

1. From clock to cloud

We're moving from being able to touch and define something permanent and precise to living with something fluid and fleeting. The cloud is no longer just a source of shade and rain. It's a source of information and ideas. The future is not a place for those who need closure and control. It's a place for those who are experimenters and explorers.

2. From fatigue to fitness

According to all our research, today's most prevalent emotion is chronic fatigue. It's taking all we have just to stay where we are. So much is coming at us so fast, it's hard to know what to focus on, never mind what to do about it. We're exhausted and we're in desperate need of more energy. We're tired of being tired. We want to feel alive and excited. So we're training like athletes. We're eating better. We're meditating. We're turning to coaches to help us thrive in every area of our lives.

3. From single to community

We're all connected all the time. We all belong to multiple

communities. We're committing to goals that are bigger than our own. Collaboration and cooperation are the order of the day. There is safety and prosperity in numbers. What's more, our communities are transcending traditional social boundaries. New insights and ideas are enrolling us in new possibilities with new partners. Empathy and reciprocation are making a comeback. It takes a global village to make us feel happy and safe.

4. From boring to fascinating

Competence alone isn't enough. We're all in competition for other people's time and attention. No matter what we do, we need to make it interesting to others. We also need to reward them for choosing us. If people enjoy being around us, they'll spend more time and money with us. Everyone is a storyteller but the stories must enrich others. We are more attracted to stories than spreadsheets – the more human the better. In the face of algorithms and automation, we crave things that are unique and specially made for us.

5. From superfluous to spartan

Whatever isn't adding value is being stripped away. Bare is beautiful. Flat is fantastic. We all need to consistently demonstrate and communicate how essential we are. The optics are as important as anything else. We also need to let go of things that are not serving us anymore. If we're not travelling light, we won't go far. The only thing that matters is how much we can help others thrive. Distraction is the enemy. Intense focus on what counts is the secret sauce. Streamline yourself to fly in the slipstreams of opportunity.

6. From old to young

Age is no longer an indication of youth. Sixty is the new 30. Seventy is the new middle age. From rockstars to thought leaders, grey power is growing. Boomers are regenerating themselves and their role in the future. They're rediscovering their mojo. They're bridging the generational divide and aligning with younger cohorts to innovate and create. All our research shows that cross-generational teams are the highest performing ones. Forever young is the mantra of the new perennials – people who never grow old.

7. From rogue to compliance

Whether we like it or not, the global meltdown has increased regulation and oversight across every industry. We're all operating in a tighter space. Either we play by the rules or we're disqualified from playing at all. It's not good enough just knowing the rules, we have to embrace them. Going rogue is not an option. But neither is resigned submission. The greater the constraints, the more creative we need to be. In a transparent world, we're all operating in a fishbowl. What happens in Vegas stays on YouTube. The great ones are models of the desired behaviour for everyone.

8. From degeneration to regeneration

Whether we're using human resources or physical resources, we need to leave the campsite in a better state than we found it. It's up to our imagination to turn scarcity into abundance. In fact, it's a necessity. Whatever we deplete, we must replenish. Our future depends on it. Success without sustainability is failure. We will be held accountable for the legacy we leave. What we do today will echo throughout the future. We're all depending on each other to make it better for the next person. This isn't altruism. It's interdependence.

9. From conformity to autonomy

From Darkest Africa to the Great White North, people are taking control of their destiny. They're making their voices heard. They're pursuing meaning, wellbeing and wealth in equal measure. The new world is rewarding those who disregard the impossible. We're such stuff as dreams are made on. We have the tools and the technology to put our thumbprint on the world. Lemmings are so 30 years ago. The cost of creation is marginal. Resources are there to be kick-started. Boundaries and barriers are only there for the faint-hearted.

10. From impersonal to personal

We're all a market of one. The new champions are customizing their message, products and services to every individual customer. And we're expressing our delight or disapproval from the digital rooftops. Everyone matters. Business is very, very personal. We're only as good as the way we make others feel. Public kudos is the ultimate currency of success. We build our personal brands one fanatical admirer at a time. Every conversation is a dialogue. Every person's opinion counts. The most important brand is our own name. Wherever you go, your network is there to welcome you in.

This book is just one way I'm aligning myself with each of these trends. It's also how I'm causing the trends. It's my way of creating the conversation. Champions are always looking for the edge. They're constantly curious. They know that the subtlest clue could help them get to the finish line first. I'm curious what trends are shaping your world and how you're leveraging them. Let me know.

IF YOU WANT TO FIND ANSWERS, LIVE THE QUESTIONS.

Questions are like spotlights that illuminate the unknown. The better the question the brighter the light. So here are eleven questions that will help illuminate your way forward:

1. What are the structural changes you're seeing in your industry?
2. What are the actions being taken by the best players in your industry?
3. What opportunities exist today that weren't there three years ago?
4. Who are the new players and what do they offer?
5. What part of your business is growing and what's dying?
6. What do you wish you did three years ago that would have put you in a better position to thrive today?
7. What must you do today to ensure you that you will be in a better position to thrive three years from now?
8. What is the biggest concern that your customers have?
9. What are the likely game-changers in the next one to three years?
10. Who are the influencers and how can you talk to them?
11. Are you connecting with a broad diversity of people or are you cloistered in your social cluster?

There may not even be answers to all these questions. The point is that just by asking them, you'll begin to see solutions you hadn't even considered.

Being compliant is a good way to be. It's reasonable, reliable, practical and steady. But if you only live by the rules, you can become pessimistic, bad-tempered, bitter and protectionist.

Compliance is the conservative part of us. It's where we're connected to others but in a quieter, consistent way that builds trust, respect and loyalty. It's also where we prove our dependability. It's the space of law and order. It's where we're careful to follow the rules and obey the process. Loose ends are tied up quickly in this space where tidiness is a virtue and stability is a goal.

Over-compliance can sink into irrelevance or obsolescence. If we become too entrenched in our ways, the desire to serve and follow can degenerate into the fear of change and reform. Rules are necessary but too many rules lead to inertia. As the game changes, so must the rules.

Faith is in this space. Our faith insulates us from the irrationality and unpredictability of life. But our faith can also close us off to the magic of other worlds and cultures. For anything to thrive, it must be open to its environment. Life cannot be quarantined.

We're at our best when we respect tradition but are prepared to break the mould. We move forward deliberately with the well-being of others in mind. We're serious but not stiflingly so. We're patient, helpful, supportive and collaborative.

Compliance is becoming even more important in a world that is a lot less fun and pleasurable than it used to be. We're living in a far more serious time. Since the great recession of 2008, the economy still hasn't returned to robust growth. Jobs are not flooding back. The global economy still appears fragile. Every day seems to bring another unwelcome shock or surprise. There is a temptation to be overly cautious and conservative. But the real need is for teamwork, camaraderie and loyalty.

I grew up in South Africa. Every business meeting there was preceded by the "tea ceremony." Attendees would share a cup of tea and share personal stories before business began. This established a climate of connection and alignment before the serious challenges were resolved. In North America today, we're lucky if we're offered a glass of water before the meeting begins and there's rarely enough time to schmooze.

Our daily test is how to build relationships of trust and loyalty with our key stakeholders. We need to make them feel an important part of our team, network or organization. We need to let people know the rules and then we need to play by them. This is the space of service and contribution. It's how we express our commitment to others and instill gratitude in them for our presence. Yup, if people are consciously grateful for our contribution, they're unlikely to dump us.

Multiple times an hour we're confronted with the temptation to become discouraged or distracted. We all need access to forces and people that will pull us back from the apocalypse. These are our anchors. They help us honour ourselves and we need to honour them. That's the meaning of engagement and loyalty.

Loyalty is declining between people, companies and brands. It's not that people are not concerned about others. It's that they're too concerned about themselves to really take great care of others. Survival means looking after "Number One." But only looking after "Number One" is the antithesis of hospitality and contribution.

In my work over 23 years with over a million people and 1000 companies in 43 countries, I've discovered there's a direct correlation between engagement and the state of the economy. Tough times equal lower engagement scores. And lower engagement scores equal lower levels of loyalty. It's hard to be fully engaged in your work when you're scared of losing it. It's even harder to step outside your box and realize that's when you need to be all-in. In a world of quasi-engaged workers, totally engaged workers rule.

Loyalty is not an obsolete concept but it's far harder to earn. We're only loyal to people or brands that spellbind us with their offering. Think of your favourite brands and service providers. The bar is being raised daily. Is your contribution doing the same?

Here's what we know for sure; it's only going to get harder. Competition will be more intense. Customers will be more demanding. The pace will be faster. The rules will be stricter. So what's the moral of the story? Make up your mental model – build a winning mindset.

BUILD A WINNING MINDSET: BE A "CERTAINIST"

We are as happy as we make up our minds to be. As Shakespeare said in Hamlet, "There is nothing either good or bad, but thinking makes it so." The world is awful or awesome depending on how we see it.

Some of us are natural optimists. The sun is always peeking through the clouds, no matter how dark. Some of us are natural pessimists. The sky could fall at any time. And some of us become optimists or pessimists depending on the circumstances.

Life is happier as an optimist but pessimists often have an enhanced sense of their realities. They're alert to the threats but often disabled by their own fatalism. They can see the train smash about to occur yet feel powerless to do anything about it. The optimist, on the other hand, can see the train coming too fast but he hopes it will stay on track.

Champions are neither optimists nor pessimists. They are "certainists." They know what is about to happen because they helped make it so. They're players on the court, not spectators in the stands. They're also certain of their ability to turn any situation to their advantage. No matter what the circumstances, they will work with them to achieve a desirable outcome.

Certainists build a mental model that guarantees victory. Losing isn't an option because it simply isn't part of the model. Certainists understand that the ends keep changing. Every outcome is the conduit to the next one. It's only the end when life literally ends.

Steve Jobs said it best, "Life can be much broader once you discover one simple fact: everything around you that you call life was made up by people that were no smarter than you and you can change it, you can influence it, you can build your own things that other people can use. Once you learn that, you'll never be the same again."

There are certain rules of the game we must embrace because we can't change them. We have to transcend just "accepting" them and learn to love them. Here are some:

- Gravity
- Physics
- The law

- Mortality
- Climate
- Time
- Body
- Human nature
- Community

Then there are rules we need to discard because they don't serve us. They may even damage us. These are the rules imposed on us by our past or our culture or the status quo. Here are some of the rules that I've discarded:

- Follow the rules
- Respect the hierarchy
- Older means slower
- People cannot change
- Everything has already been thought of
- The world is a mean and nasty place
- The odds are stacked against me
- I'm too small to make a difference
- Generations don't understand each other
- Demography is destiny
- Tradition is everything
- Be careful what you say
- Life is fragile

- Conflict is inevitable
- Life is unfair

Think about the rules that have governed your life so far. What are the limits you've set for yourself or other people have set for you? What constraints could you vaporize in a heartbeat? What bogeymen do you need to slay? What traditions do you need to transcend? What habits do you need to liberate yourself from?

Begin by identifying just one constraint, tradition or habit that you can transcend. As Tony Schwartz, CEO of The Energy Project, wrote in The New York Times (November 29, 2015), "We humans have a very limited reservoir of will and discipline. We're far more likely to succeed by trying to change one behavior at a time, ideally at the same time every day, so that it becomes a habit, requiring less and less energy to sustain." The one behaviour I've changed is procrastination – especially when it comes to writing. That's how this book was completed. What's yours?

Over the past 16 years, The Environics/Lipkin Behavioural Research has discovered that "The New Champions" create a winning mindset. I call it the **"Dynamic Diamond"** because it comprises four essential elements that are always in motion:

The Dynamic Diamond

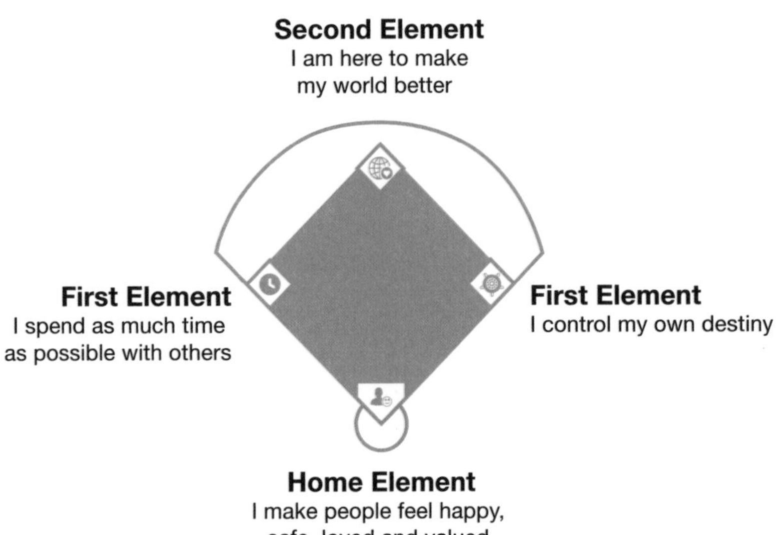

First Element: I control my own destiny.

I have the power to determine my own destiny: this is called confidence. It's the belief in your ability to recreate oneself and your future. It's the capacity to build a life that is fulfiling. It's knowledge the "system" is there to be leveraged to your advantage. In short, the locus of control is within you. The power comes from within.

Second Element: I am here to make my world better.

I am here to make the world better: this is called idealism. It's the enduring commitment to the ideal of mutual contribution and social enhancement. It's the antithesis of "just being out for number one." It's the belief you can be altruistic and capitalistic as the same time. In short, it's an understanding that to be worthy of your gifts, your have to use them to benefit the world.

Third Element: I spend as much time as possible with others.

I am a highly social being: I will spend as much time as I can with other people. This is called connection. It's a visceral joy derived from the sharing of experiences, information and stories with other people. It's a knowledge that the most powerful learning is through human interaction. It's a belief that it takes a village to raise yourself to the highest level. It's a love of diversity and a consuming curiosity about how others think, live, work and play. It is best expressed by an old African proverb: a person is a person because of other people.

Home Element: I make people feel happy, safe, loved and valued.

I make people feel happy, safe, loved and valued. This is called true-success. This is the elixir. It's the power to attract allies and influence people. It's where the all the pleasure and the treasure are buried.

I've discovered that 100 percent of people want to be happy. One hundred percent of people want to feel safe. One hundred percent of people want love. One hundred percent of people hate to be disappointed. One hundred percent of people want to be admired. One hundred percent of people hate being taken for granted.

We're only as good as the way we make others feel. Personality and emotion are closely related. Our personality is the sum total of the emotions others associate with us.

Think about your best friend. Describe their personality. Are they likeable? Trustworthy? Caring? Supportive? Giving? Entertaining?

If we like them, they're likeable. If we trust them, they're trustworthy. If they support us, they're supportive. If they give to us, they're giving. If they entertain us, they're entertaining. In other words, our feelings towards them are how we define the kind of person they are.

At a certain level, we all want the same things from others. These are the basic hygiene factors of trust, openness, caring, understanding and empathy. But at a higher level, we all have unique needs. We want to be transported to an emotional state that yields the highest pleasure. Anyone or anything that can do that for us becomes indispensable.

Emotion *is* the message. We talk to transfer feelings as much as information. The *how* and the *what* give others the *why*. Unless we make people feel happy, safe, loved and valued, the data are diminished. People forget the facts. But when it comes to feelings, elephants have got nothing on humans – we never forget our feelings.

We can force people to do something, but we can't force them to do it well. Survival is mandatory. Inspiration is optional. Survival pays the rent. Inspiration owns the house. Survival means getting through the day. Inspiration means making someone else's day.

When we feel happy, safe, loved and valued, we're comforted and inspired. We feel like we're home. We're complete. We can take on anything because we feel empowered. That's why the "home element" is "make people feel happy, safe, loved and valued." These emotions are all intertwined. They're also all under siege by the environment, that is becoming scarier by the day.

Over the past five years, one of the strongest life-trends tracked by The Environics Social Values Monitor is "fear of violence."

It's grown by 51 percent since 2009. Urban terror is a common phenomenon. From New York and Boston to Ottawa and Toronto to London, Paris and Sydney, bad people can do bad things at any time.

Along with the fear of violence is a decline in appetite for risk. Appetite for risk has declined by 19 percent since 2009. The global financial meltdown has taken its toll. Economic volatility has magnified our fear of failure. Probable penalties outweigh potential payouts. Playing it safe is the new insurance.

The desire for "personal control" has increased by 27 percent since 2009. That means striving to organize and control the direction of your future, even when it seems like there are forces beyond your immediate control. Perception is reality. Against all odds, we want to believe we can control our lives. So we build our castles and construct moats around us to keep the bogeymen at bay.

Another Environics Social Values life-trend is "Aversion to Complexity." It's grown by 37 percent since 2009. The more complex and matrixed the world becomes, the more we feel threatened by change and crave simplicity. Across all demographics, we're seeing "retromania." This is nostalgia that's not even based on past experience. It's based on an idealized version of the past: connections were personal; friends were real; interaction was actual; goods were handmade and hand delivered; life was affordable; the pace was manageable; the future was clear; you believed in something and you belonged somewhere.

The next Environics Social Values life-trend is "Emotional Control." This trend has risen by 39 percent since 2009. It's the inclination to prioritize reason as a principal way of understanding life. It's the desire to keep your emotional life "on an even keel." It's a reluctance to give up control or even express our feelings. This trend aligns with the decline of another trend called "Intuition and Impulse." This is the unwillingness to be impulsive and spontaneous. It's also a resistance to change. When the outside world appears more hostile, we're less willing to "just do it" or "roll the dice." We don't want to make costly mistakes and that can turn out to be very expensive.

One more life-trend I'll share with you is called "Vitality." It's the antidote to the other trends. It's grown by 55 percent since 2009. It's a sense you have a great deal of energy and are deeply connected to this energy. It's the belief that you have more vigour and initiative than other people. It's the rocket fuel of personal success.

So think about your interpretation of the "Dynamic Diamond." How can you control your own destiny? How can you make your world better? How can you spend more time with others? And how can you make others feel happy, safe, loved and valued?

Write down your thoughts right here, right now.

I control my destiny by…

____

____

____

____

I make my world better through...

I will spend more time with others by...

I make others feel happy, safe, loved and valued through...

BUILD THE YIN AND YANG OF YOUR "PERSONAL BRAND PLAN"

Your personal brand is a marriage of yin and yang; the internal and external. It's the fusion between your function and other people's feelings about your function. It is literally other people's opinions of your worth to them.

Amazon CEO Jeff Bezos says, "your brand is what other people say about you when you're not in the room." Their perception of your contribution is their reality of who you are. The real prize is to live the perception we want other people to have of us.

How many times have you learned someone's opinions of you were completely different to your self-image? How do you feel when it happens to you? Surprised? Frustrated? Puzzled? Amused? Upset? All of the above?

At first, I'm always stunned when others see me differently to the way I see myself. Then I think about the way I've behaved. I look at myself from their point of view and I understand them. It's often uncomfortable to see what others have seen. It's hard to acknowledge our unappealing qualities. But it's always enlightening, especially when I can find the amusing aspects of the disparity.

As someone who has to compete fiercely for every assignment, I'm in constant sell mode. My most successful moments are when I convince others that I am the best at what I do. To convince others means to cause them to believe firmly in the truth of something. At that moment, my belief about myself and other people's beliefs about me fuse together. We create a shared reality that creates an extraordinary future. Sometimes that fusion happens serendipitously. But most times, it requires a conscious personal brand plan.

A great personal brand is best described by the writer, James A. Michener, as a "Master in the art of living." He states, "The master in the art of living makes little distinction between his work and his play, his labour and his leisure, his mind and his body, his information and his recreation, his love and his religion. He hardly knows which is which. He simply pursues his *vision of excellence* at whatever he does, leaving others to decide whether he is working or playing. To him he's always doing both."

A personal brand plan is your vision of excellence that enables you to convince others that you are the best at what you do. It enables you to tune out the distractions and tune into your unique power. It's simple and succinct. It comprises six steps – what, why, how, where, who, when:

1. **What: your desired outcome in the next year.**

What is the specific result that will make the next year the best year of your career? How can you express it in a way that excites both you and your stakeholders? Remember: the difference between a vision and a hallucination is that other people can see your vision.

Here is mine. You'll see that I have written it in the past tense. In my mind, it has already happened. I am in lag time. The fact that you're reading this is proof that it has occurred:

> Mike Lipkin is a brand that has motivated 100,000 people to buy a copy of "The Checklist of Champions" in the year following its publication. In the same period, 100 of those people hired Mike to work with their teams around the world. As a result of these experiences, Mike has multiplied his capacity and reputation as a catalyst for the world's most demanding professionals.

Now write yours:

2. Why: your passion and your purpose.

What do you love to do? What's the reason you do it? What gives you the inspiration and stamina to achieve your desired outcome? How can you declare it in way that lights you up every time you read it? Here's mine:

> Mike Lipkin's mission is to excite people into action. His passion is to enable people to achieve results they would not have otherwise achieved. He savours the kudos of clients who share their gratitude with him. He believes he was born to inspire people.
>
> He loves the thrill of the crowd, the revelling in the kudos, the delight of connecting with strangers who become instant friends and the excitement of being part of big moments with big consequences. He wants to be a sought-after personal brand that makes people happy, successful and remarkable. He also wants to be attractive to others so they want to be around him.

Now write yours:

____

____

____

____

____

____

____

____

3. How: your strategy for achieving your what and your why.

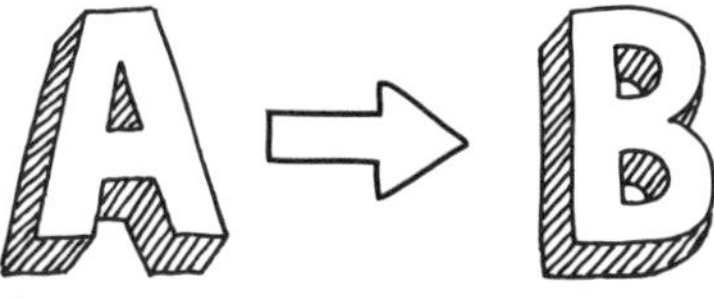

How can you define your method for success in a simple statement? How can you leverage your greatest strengths? What's your secret sauce? How could you share it with others so they get it immediately? Here's mine:

> Mike Lipkin is the most enthusiastic person he knows. His greatest strength is his ability to communicate his enthusiasm to energize others to achieve results. He seizes every opportunity to build his mental and physical capacity to transfer excitement and possibility to others. He lives young.

Now write yours:

---

4. Where: the arena in which you play.

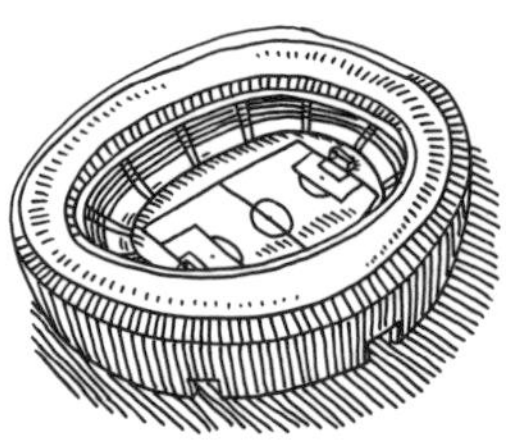

What's the space in which you specialize? Where do you earn the highest return on your energy? What do you focus on for maximum impact? Here's mine:

> Mike Lipkin serves people and organizations that want to be "best of breed." They're already good but they want to be great. Mike focuses his efforts on bespoke assignments customized to key factors driving the success of his individual and corporate clients. Mike works anywhere in the world with any industry or function as long as it's legal. Champions are boundary-less.

Now write yours:

____

____

____

____

____

____

____

____

5. Who: the people who are central to your success.

Who are the people that comprise your network? Which people can become mobilizers of opportunity for you? Who are the most talented performers you need to align with? Here are mine:

> Mike Lipkin has aligned himself with the best research and strategic advisors in Canada – The Environics Research Group. He partners with the leading speaking bureaus in North America to deepen his penetration of the corporate sector.

He employs the most talented freelance designers, web developers, video producers and publishers to package his content. He connects with key opinion leaders across all industries to earn credibility with marquee clients. He surrounds himself with people who are plugged in and ready to play.

Now write yours:

____

____

____

____

____

____

____

____

6. When: the cadence of your activities.

What's the cycle of your connections? How often do you need to be reaching out to your clients and network? What's the ideal rhythm of your communication? Here's mine:

Mike Lipkin creates a new book every two years. He produces a new program every six months. He communicates with his entire network via a viral campaign every month. He calls the top 300 people in his network every six weeks.

Now write yours:

____

____

____

____

____

____

____

____

A PLAN IS ONLY AS GOOD AS THE PEOPLE YOU ENROL IN THE PLAN

It's your network that makes the plan work. They must be touched, moved and inspired to help you execute your plan. If you cannot incite others into action, your plan isn't worth a damn.

The early 20th century architect and urban planner Daniel Burnham said, "Make no little plans; they have no magic to stir men's blood and probably themselves will not be realized. Make big plans; aim high in hope and work. Let your watchword be order and your beacon beauty."

Test your plan on your confidantes. Evaluate its capacity to stir their blood. Then, share your plan with your wider circle of associates and peers. The best indicator of success is the number of people who volunteer their time, effort or resources to turn the plan into reality.

You're reading these words because of the amazing people who committed to purchasing and advocating this book to their communities. They expressed their passion for the content and promised me they would promote it. Then they followed through.

As importantly, their encouragement prohibited me from giving up on the plan. When people commit to buying thousands of books in advance of its publication, it's impossible not to publish it.

So let your plan out to play. There are far more people who will champion you than cheapen you. Their insights will embolden you. In turn, your plan will embolden them to take action. I enrolled people in my plan because my plan enrolled them into creating a plan of their own.

The best promotion begins with self-promotion. Before you can create champions of your plan, you have to champion your plan. In order to win, you have to create beauty in the eye of the beholder.

How to pursue awesome - the story of Jimmy John's Gourmet Sandwiches.

The ultimate test of enrolment is whether you can persuade people to invest their life in your plan. That's literally the goal of franchise operations. One of the most successful franchises in the U.S. is Jimmy John's Gourmet Sandwiches. It was founded in 1983 by Jimmy John Liautaud and is headquartered in Champaign, Illinois.

In 30 years, the company has grown to more than 2000 locations in 43 states.

In 2016, Entrepreneur Magazine rated Jimmy John's Gourmet Sandwiches as the number one franchise in America based on factors like financial strength and stability, growth rate and size of the system.

Here's how Jimmy John Liautaud describes his journey and his "plan":

> "I graduated from Elgin Academy High School in June of 1982. I graduated second to last in my high school class, so my options for college were slim to none.
>
> My real love was Chicago street food, specifically Chicago Style Vienna Hot Dogs, like Portillo's serves. The summer that I graduated high school, I visited many hot dog stands in the Chicago suburbs and created a menu from my research as well as a list of the equipment I would need to open.
>
> I went to the used restaurant equipment district in Chicago to buy my equipment, but found out that I needed about $45K to open a hot dog stand. My budget was $25K so that was out of the question. I then stumbled on to Booby's Sandwiches in Carbondale, Illinois. When I walked in, I saw a refrigerator, a meat slicer and a cash register. Way less equipment than the hot dog stand required. From there I switched to sandwiches and never looked back.
>
> Next, I had to learn to bake bread so I checked-out books from

the library. I baked and I baked until I got it right. That recipe evolved into the Jimmy John's bread of today. From there I bought deli meats and I started working on a menu.

By August of 1982, I had four sandwiches for my menu. I had two cousins at Eastern Illinois University in Charleston, Illinois so I chose to look there for my first location. I found a site, it was a two-car garage that had been remodeled into a pizza joint but it had closed down. The location was surrounded by bars. Perfect! Students drink, they get hungry, I'd stay open late and I would feed them.

I opened in January 1983. My dad was my partner, he owned 48 percent and I owned 52 percent. The first year we did $155,000 in sales and made $40,000 profit that I split with my dad. The second year, we did $188,000 in sales and made $50,000 profit. I worked seven days a week, about 15 hours a day and my salary was $200 per week, which equated to about two bucks an hour.

In May of 1986 I bought out my dad and Jimmy John's was all mine.

By 1994 I had 10 sub shops, I was doing my own accounting, I paid for everything C.O.D. and I had no debt. I was rolling! Ten years, 10 stores and no debt! America, what a country!

By 2002, I had 160 stores open but 70 were failing. I stopped selling franchises that year and my President and I went on a mission to turn around those 70 failing stores. They weren't following my system and weren't into the restaurant lifestyle. It took 18 months, we turned around 63 of them and closed seven.

I learned a lot from that experience so I changed the rules for allowing people to buy into my system as a franchisee. I explained how tough running a Jimmy John's can be. I explained the long hours, the unforgiving weather, the late nights, the weekends and all of the sacrifices that go along with the industry. I made it tough for people to get into the system.

I had learned early that this business is not sexy, it's hard work, it's long hours and it can be brutal. If you get past that, it's one of the most rewarding lifestyles. Everyday transactions take place by choice and both sides win. It's called free enterprise. I liked that.

I worked late nights and weekends, took the toughest jobs for myself, including cleaning the toilets. We installed a stereo system, played great music and created a very cool work environment. The kids who worked for me worked their butts off, but they got a kick out of my leadership by example style, so they asked their friends to come work for me.

We started sharing 25 percent of the profit with our managers and that incentive exploded the store sales. As we grew, many of the rock stars were promoted from the Jimmy John's sub shops to become my executives. My President was a Sandwich Maker in 2000 and today he implements my vision and runs this giant company. The stores are a launching pad for people who want to change their lives.

The culture is so deep that it has become a very attractive place to work, to grow and to win in life. It makes me feel good that I developed a system where people can grow, develop valuable skills and learn to lead. This system teaches people to be proactive, to budget and to save their money. Today, much of the head office was former Sandwich Makers, Delivery, Drivers, Store Managers or Guerilla Markers. Many of our franchisees were once employees.

We are very close in our company; we treat others as we would like to be treated. We take care of each other and it's been incredibly rewarding. I never intended for this company to be as big as it is today. It's simply a byproduct of a disciplined, systemized concept that is effectively audited and operated by people who care. It's about the pursuit of awesome, it's about helping people help themselves; it's about transparency. It's real and it's very, very hard, but it's what we love, it's all we know.

Who We Let Do This Deal

Think you have what it takes?

1. You have to have the cash.
2. Real passion for my brand. If you don't dig it as much as we all dig it, this brand is not for you!
3. You've got to be a good, hard-working, well-intended individual, who respects yourself and others.
4. You've got to take specific, detailed, & disciplined direction extremely well.
5. You can't be a criminal.
6. You've got to love life, kids, music, dancing, your grandparents & sandwiches.

7. Last, be excited to work harder than you ever have in your life."

You may be a sandwich maker, a financial advisor or a software designer, but you need a plan that you promote with your unique gusto and flair. Write your "Jimmy John" story and share it with others. You'll be amazed at who will step up to your plate.

How to differentiate your brand in a brutally competitive travel environment: Icelandair uses the buddy system to make friends and win over travellers.

In April 2016, Icelandair offered a "stopover buddy" to be your free travel guide for up to 24 hours in Iceland on your way to 26 spots in Europe. The "buddy" is an Icelandair employee who could be anyone from the CEO to a pilot or check-in agent. The buddy crafts an itinerary around your passions. These could include themes like lifestyle, food, nature or adventure.

That's how to enrol people in your plan: come up with an amazing idea. Sell it to your own team members. Empower them to play their role to perfection. Then sell it to prospects.

AS THINGS CHANGE, CHANGE YOUR PLAN

The best thing about the future is no one has been there. At best, anticipation is an approximate art. Your plan is a discipline channelling your efforts but it's only as good as the course corrections you make.

As someone who has flown over three million miles in his career, I spend a lot of time at 30,000 feet. But on any given flight, the ability for an airplane to go from one place to another has almost nothing to do with its ability to stay on course. The plane does have a course heading it follows, but on average, any airplane will actually be off course for 95 percent of its flight.

The computers on board will tell the airplane it has veered off course. Sophisticated systems then allow the plane to make a correction. As the plane corrects, other factors may now place the plane off course by a few degrees and once again the plane makes a correction. So for an airplane to get to its destination, it requires an ability to constantly evaluate its position (relative to where it might want to be) and be able to make necessary corrections.

Additional factors related to weather, national security or migrating birds, may pose challenges to the plane and it will be required to take this additional input into account to make the best choices for correcting. In many cases, the plane must abandon its flight path altogether, occasionally causing it to venture out into unknown territories, often due to unforeseen circumstances.

As people, our course headings are complicated by the fact that our destinations have never been reached before. They may not even exist. The course corrections we make are related as much to our internal geography as external circumstances.

As a strategic coach, I often work with people whose priorities change over time. They discover things about themselves that make their previous trajectory less attractive or other avenues more desirable. The problem is they don't change their plan to enable course correction. They end up with a faulty GPS that takes them in the wrong direction.

So here are my questions to you: Are you course correcting in real time? Is your plan aligned with your internal and external realities? Are you letting go of what doesn't serve you and embracing what does?

I recently flew from Toronto to Tucson with a connection in Denver for a speaking engagement. My departure was delayed because of weather so I arrived at the departure gate in Denver with just minutes to spare. The ground attendant informed me I was too late and boarding was already complete. Yet the doors were still open. I could see the airplane. I could also see the pain I would experience if I missed my engagement because I couldn't get there on time. So I summoned up all my charisma and charm. I begged the ground attendant to let me on the flight. She looked at me with a mixture of amusement and pity. Then she asked me a simple question: do you have any baggage? "No," I replied and she allowed me to board. So what's the moral of the story: let go of your baggage. Travel light. And get to where you need to go – with a little help from your fellow human beings.

Now that you identify as a champion, dream like a champion and plan like a champion, it's time to explore what it means to *feel* like a champion.

4

FEEL LIKE A CHAMPION

FIRST, CHAMPIONS WILL BE COURAGEOUS

SECOND, CHAMPIONS WILL BE EXCITED

THIRD, CHAMPIONS WILL BE ENGAGED

FOURTH, CHAMPIONS WILL BE AT EASE

FIFTH, CHAMPIONS WILL BE GENEROUS

FEEL LIKE A CHAMPION

Your emotional state says more about you than you can ever say. It determines whether you're a master or a monster, a wizard or a wimp, a catalyst or a coward. What's more, your emotional state also brings out the best or the worst in others.

Let me ask you, have you ever been so good in a meeting you amazed yourself? Have you ever said something so sublime that even you were shaken by your brilliance? On the other hand, have you ever just coasted through a meeting and felt really crappy about your performance afterwards? Even worse, have you made other people miserable in a meeting because of your negativity?

Here's Lipkin's silver bullet for becoming a champion: understand the emotion in which you perform best. Then intentionally step into it. Flip your emotional switch whenever the moment demands it. It can be done and you can do it. It requires self-awareness, technique and practice. But the good news is that you can experiment with it multiple times a day.

What is your emotion for top performance? It may be calmness, confidence, fear, comfort, ease, love, generosity, anger, courage, happiness, exhilaration or excitement.

In my case, it's definitely excitement. I must be eagerly anticipating whatever happens next. I must be turned on by the prospect of making a difference, stretching myself to the limit, meeting someone incredible, learning something brand new, going on an adventure or spending time with people I love.

In many cases, those situations are real. I've designed my life to maximize the frequency of those experiences. It's easy for me to get excited when I'm confronted by exciting moments, just like it's easy to be happy when you're surrounded by happiness.

The challenge is to be excited when I'm not immersed in an exciting environment. In fact, the real power comes from being excited when I'm in a situation that really sucks. Here are just a few of the situations that really suck for me:

- Being in an argument with my wife.
- Talking to someone who believes that I don't get it.
- Losing a gig that I really wanted to win.
- Being exhausted when I still have a huge task ahead of me.
- Being taken by negative surprise – whether it's losing a relationship, money or business.
- Getting sick.
- Suffering from writer's block
- Believing I have taken on too much work in the time available to me.

- Not being "on" when I need to be "on."

Those are the moments when I need to conjure up my feelings of excitement. I need to find or make a way to become excited by some aspect of my situation. And when the student is ready, the teacher appears. Whatever you look for, you tend to find. As long as I remember to hunt for excitement, I know I will find it. And the more I do it, the better I become.

I even verbalize my thoughts, "What I find exciting about this is…" Or, "The thing that fascinates me about this moment is…" Just saying the words, triggers my thoughts into action. The word is the seed of the deed.

The language of touch.

> **"The emotional quality of gentle nurturing touch is a very important feeling that underpins a lot of social interaction. The reward system in our brains promotes behaviour that is beneficial to survival. Looking back in evolution, it became apparent that organisms that work together were far more successful. To promote that togetherness, there was a need to promote the value of close contact."**
> Francis McGlone, neuroscientist, Liverpool John Moores University, England

Touch down. Touch up. Touch off. A touch of class. A pat on the back. A helping hand. A warm hug. A firm grip. A strong support. A reassuring presence. A close friend. An electric smile. A magnetic personality. A stroke of luck. A gentle reminder. A soft whisper. A hard stop. A smooth ride. A pleasurable feeling. A cool look. A hot outfit. A tear jerker.

Welcome to the language of touch. It's the closest I can come to hugging you right now. I want to reach out and draw you in. I want to fire you up so you can bring the heat. I'm excited to talk to you. This is fantastic. Can you feel me?

Words don't just describe reality; they create the reality they describe. We live inside the words we use. They're the way we make sense of the world. Great lives come from great stories and great stories come from great lives. This is not big talk; it's great talk. If you want to experience something great, you have to use the word "great" otherwise you'll experience something else. If you want to feel joy, delight or ecstasy, you need express your joy, delight or ecstasy. Just as an artist needs colours to create her masterpiece, you need words to create yours.

First and foremost, we are emotional beings. The starting point is to realize things are never just things. They have a unique meaning to us that comes from their "emotional tagging." An emotional tag is the way we file things in our brain and body. It's the feeling we experienced when we first encountered them or something similar to them. We feel things first then we think, talk or act accordingly. Motion is driven by emotion.

The truth is we're driven by things we don't fully understand and can't even control. Our minds comprise different layers, most of which are subconscious. In fact, our conscious mind is like the bark on a tree. It's even called the neocortex. "Neo" means new because this is the newest part of the human brain to evolve in the generation of conscious thought and language.

Most of our decision-making is at a more primitive, even molecular level. Everything from the cause of fear to the chemical exchange of data between our cells is beyond the scope of our conscious will. So, next time you find yourself doing things or feeling things you don't understand, make peace with it. The answer will percolate to the surface when it's ready.

People assume the real drivers of their decisions are rational. But the real drivers are "E-Rational." E-rational isn't irrational. It's the fusion of emotion and rational. It's the collection of feelings, relationships, perceptions, values, deep beliefs and biochemistry that make up who we are.

Emotions are the conscious awareness of the body's reaction to internal and external events. They occur when we become aware of our body's pattern of decision-making. Emotions are generated by historical associations. Certain patterns are hardwired into us culturally, genetically and individually. The more tuned in we are to our emotions, the more consciousness we can bring to our decisions. And the greater our influence over them.

Reason without emotion doesn't work. Without recognizing our body's reactions, we have no guide to what decision will be best for us. And the truth contains far too much information to make a completely rational decision anyway. Think about it: we do a Google search that gets millions of hits yet we only look at the first page because that's all we have time for. No one has the capacity to sift through all the salient information available.

Understanding the concept of e-rational offers you a fast track to effective decision-making. E-rational is the new rational because rational is always embedded with emotion. Think about how you feel about anyone who says, "Let's all be rational here." It's never an appropriate thing to say because it's impossible.

Champions touch people both literally and figuratively.

Watch the end of any game. The language of winning is physical. It's laughter, embrace, exclamation, joy, high-fives and partying. The language of losing is lethargy, futility, tears, despair and isolation. Winning brings people together. It reinforces their faith in each other. Losing splits people apart. When we win, we look forward to winning the next game. When we lose, we fear losing again.

Our approach varies by culture, gender and personality. For example, during conversations Italians will touch each other more than Canadians. Women will touch each other much more than men. Artists will touch each other more than accountants. Extroverts will touch each other more than introverts. And happy people touch each other more than unhappy people.

The language of touch is the language of contact and togetherness. It's the language of outreach. It transcends the functional role of transferring information to also transferring emotions. Indeed, the real reason why we communicate may be the transfer of feelings not facts. Without the necessary emotions, there is no impetus to act.

Think about why you're reading this book. What motivated you to choose it? What do you hope to gain from it? Why is that important to you? Who will you share it with? How are you feeling right now?

Everything comes wrapped in feelings. It's the feelings that open up our ability to absorb anything else. We feel, therefore we listen, look, learn or run away.

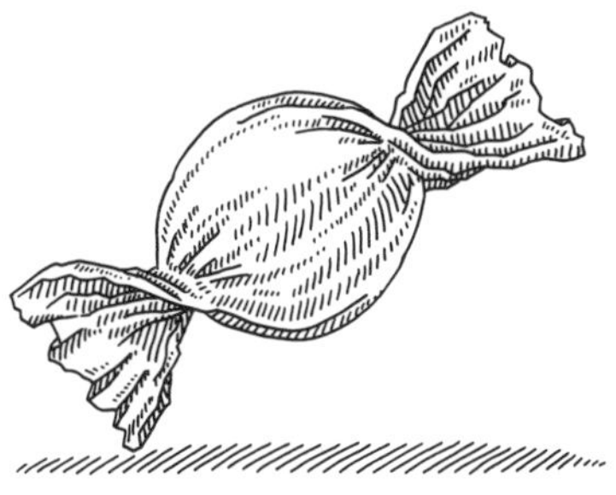

As a professional motivator, I specialize in touch. I am a sculptor of people's spirit. I know that a single sentence can make or break the spell. I have to get the audience to like me before they can like my content. They have to feel comfortable and excited, relaxed and tense, familiar and new. My purpose in every session is to engage and enthuse people into action.

Your purpose may be different in many ways but it's exactly the same in one really important way: you want people to do something as a result of interacting with you. Maybe you just want a reaction. Or maybe you want them to want you. Maybe you want them to be nice to you. Or you want them to work with you, play with you, serve you or support you. If you know what you want, you're far more likely to get it.

Champions have the "Magic Touch." The Magic Touch is one's unique ability to thrill people by doing something remarkably well. Let me repeat that: The Magic Touch is one's unique ability to thrill people by doing something remarkably well. The emotional impact is what really counts. That's how The Magic Touch creates "magic moments." A magic moment is that instant "WOW" when you make someone happy, excited, passionate, enthusiastic, ecstatic, courageous, fulfilled, joyous or powerful.

I am going to go Michelangelo and Sistine Chapel on you here. When you apply The Magic Touch you close the gap between what is and what can be. Your touch is what puts people in touch with their potential. And they're inspired to touch it forward. It becomes a never-ending chain of divine consequences. Just remember, one sentence from you can be a life sentence for someone else.

The highest expression of appreciation is when someone tells you, "I'm deeply touched."

It's when they feel your contribution at a heart level. It's when they show it's a joy to receive your joy. It's when your inspiration inspires them. It's when you demonstrate in the crucial moments that it's all about them.

When The Magic Touch creates a magic moment, it's always an unforgettable moment for the person experiencing it, especially when the rest of their life is full of humdrum, mediocre and stressful moments. The Magic Touch is the difference between a smile that lights someone up from the inside and a shrug weighing them even further down.

In the age of the machine, "The Magic Touch" is even more powerful because it can only be delivered by a human being.

The Magic Touch is augmented by machines, but it can't be automated by machines. As Thomas Davenport and Julia Kirby write in the June 2015 issue of the Harvard Business Review,

"Automation starts with a baseline of what people do in a given job and subtracts from that. It deploys computers to chip away at the tasks humans perform as soon as those tasks can be codified. Augmentation, in contrast, means starting with what humans do today and figuring out how that work could be deepened rather than diminished by a greater use of machines."

In the same issue, Andrew McAfee is quoted as saying "This era will be better for the simple reason that, thanks to digital technologies, we'll be able to produce more: more health care, more education, more entertainment and more of all the other material goods and services we value. And we'll be able to extend this bounty to more and more people around the world while treading lightly on the planet's resources. "

According to Erik Brynjolfsson, faculty member at MIT Sloan School of Management, "this is an opportunity for entrepreneurs to think of ways of using humans in new applications, combining them with technology. We call that racing with machines as opposed to racing against them." That's what we're doing right here. We're racing with machines to distribute this message as fast and far as we can. We're scaling The Magic Touch to enable thousands to reach out and up – including you.

The ultimate question raised by Brynjolsson is, "How can I have this machine and this human work together to do something never done before and create something that will be more valuable in the marketplace?"

That's my challenge to you: what can you do today with your technology that's never done before and create something that will be more valuable in the marketplace? That's a goal worth striving for, right?

Whatever you want from people, you need to feel it first. Others will mirror your emotions. Champions move people, both figuratively and literally. My greatest challenge as a motivational speaker is when I'm in front on an audience that is comprised of "prisoners" and "skeptics." The former are people who do not want to be in the room but they feel like they have been forced there. The latter are people who either don't trust what I'm saying or don't believe it's true. In both cases, I'm confronted with emotions like dislike, fear, resentment, anger, frustration and boredom. It's very easy for me to succumb to their emotional vortex. But I'm paid to pull them out of the rabbit hole into the light.

I need to step into the light even before I step onto the stage. I need to elevate my mindset and mood to lift everyone around me. So I visualize my audience responding enthusiastically. I think about the impact I can have on their lives. I watch and listen to great speakers before I begin speaking. I read motivational quotes. I remember how I've thrived in similar moments. And the final thing that I do before I get onto the stage is CIA – "celebrate in advance." I feel the way I will feel when I get a standing ovation – the pride, the joy, the recognition, the love and the fulfilment.

That's my ritual before every single talk. That's how I reach for the brass ring. That's how I turn prisoners and skeptics into students and champions. The best words I can ever hear from someone are

"I didn't want to be here. But now I'm so glad I was. I never saw things that way before. I feel so much better about my life." What are the best words that you want to hear from others? And how do you need to feel to move people to say them?

Negative emotions precipitate the action of withdrawal or moving away. Positive emotions cause engagement and attraction. But here's the key point: we are moved more by negative emotions than positive ones. So the ratio of positive emotions to negative ones needs to be about three to one. The moment we get more than 25 percent negative responses, it can neutralize all the positive ones.

Intense emotions are intoxicating. Literally. They can exhilarate, energize and enthuse us to great heights. Or they can paralyze, poison or plunge us into great despair. Depression or shock has a great pull even though it may not make rational sense. One person's "tiny" may be another person's "huge." Depression also inhibits or unleashes hormones that govern our mood. What begins as a whimper can culminate in torment.

Excitement or terror, on the other hand, generate adrenaline that electrifies us into action. It can also be damaging to the body if it stays for too long. That means the body has to get rid of it quickly. A state of excitement has to be short lived. It comes and it goes. That's why we need to keep generating this emotion for others and ourselves.

Excitement is fast. Depression is slow. We're catapulted into the former and trapped in the latter. Either way, it's the body's response to a compelling call. We need to listen to it. Right now, I'm excited to be writing these words. I could also be overwhelmed by the amount of effort and time required to complete this book. I choose to be drawn towards excitement not overwhelm. That's why you're reading these words.

The comfort zone is our safe space, but it can also be a prison.

The comfort zone is seductive. It's the promise of stability. It's what we know. It's what we rely on. It's what we want to preserve and protect. It's reasonable. It's compromise. It's predictable. It's moderation. It's a constant in a constantly changing world. It's the shelter in the storm.

The comfort zone is also a kind of prison. It's a place we're afraid to break out of. But it's also far less secure than it may have been in the past. In the past, we could have consoled ourselves with the belief that dull and boring could mean safe and secure. We could have lived with the belief that the purgatory of Monday-to-Friday was an acceptable price to pay for the contentment of Saturday and Sunday. The mantra was "I don't like what I'm doing but I know how to do it and at least I know it's safe."

No more. The new kind of comfort zone is armed with the Sword of Damocles hanging over our heads. It's ridden with angst. The mantra has changed to "I don't like what I'm doing but maybe it will all change immediately and I could be fired tomorrow." Whatever work you do, "safe" has left the building. We may not like what we do for a living, we may not even like how we live, but we cannot hide behind the smokescreen, "At least it's secure." The new spartanism is unforgiving. Even those paying their way may not get to stay. So come out, come out wherever you are. To break out of the comfort zone, we first have to confront we're stuck in it

– with no mitigating circumstances.

Whenever I hear the phrase, “I don’t like it but at least it’s…” I know I’m in the presence of someone who is hoodwinking himself. He’s taking his own poison. Don’t get me wrong. I’m not stating that there’s an easy way out of the comfort zone. I’m not even saying that the comfort zone isn’t an acceptable place to be – for a while. I *am* saying there are shades of comfort zone, from healthy to toxic. It’s about understanding how long you’ve been there before you move out. The comfort zone is a place to rent not own.

Think about it: if all I told you was “Jane is a relaxed, down-to-earth person open to new ideas,” wouldn’t you immediately be attracted to Jane? On the other hand, if I told you “Jane is stuck in her comfort zone and scared to explore new horizons,” you may not be drawn to her unless she awakened your fraternal love or instincts as a Good Samaritan.

Too much time in the comfort zone can make you numb. And numb can be its own kind of pain. After a while, you don’t even notice your detachment. That’s when the antidote needs to be extreme. And that’s when the effort to reclaim your vitality needs to be acute and oversize.

I know. Ironically, I became a coach and motivator because in my lifetime, I have experienced three episodes of clinical depression. It took both pharmaceutical intervention and electro convulsive therapy to restore my mental wellbeing. Unless you’ve been there, it’s impossible to understand how intractable this state can be.

Acute distress demands immediate treatment. If we’re smart, we’ll seek the right help or talk to the right people and find the right solution. If we’re not, we’ll try to self-medicate through drink, drugs or distraction. Either way, the problem will be addressed. The first way may solve it. The second way may make it worse, which will force us to revert to the first way.

It's the low level of chronic anxiety that's even more dangerous. That's when we're getting through the day in a state of repressed fear. It's when we're living with a nagging sense of self-doubt, on the edge of an imagined abyss we could fall into at any moment. This is when we become a breakdown-waiting-to-happen. It's when a seemingly innocuous event tips us into a tantrum or turmoil.

This low level of chronic anxiety also produces an internal chemical reaction that inflicts low-grade damage to our system. It etches lines on our face and even affects our posture over time. We call it the "posture of doubt." It's a facial expression or a physical inclination that communicates internal uncertainty and concern. We can read people's mindset by their face and stance. Emotion comes from motion. Either we feel their unease and angst or we sense their optimism and appetite for life. What do people feel or sense around you? What do the lines on your face say about you? Which way are you leaning? Are you a breakdown-waiting-to-happen? Or are you a lightning rod for possibility?

Hey, life is serious business but when we take ourselves too seriously we cannot be champions. Champions escape their comfort zones by entering the "play zone." They understand that fun is the lubrication enabling all the other pieces of their life to work together. So let's go there now.

The "Play Zone" is the space of pleasure, desire, experimentation and entertainment. It makes you happy but if you go too far, it will make you miserable.

We are shaped by our desires. We're formed by what we lust after. We mould ourselves into the kind of person who will attract what we want most.

For me, it's the thrill of the crowd; it's the revelling in the kudos, it's the joy of connecting with strangers who become instant friends, it's the excitement of being part of big moments that have big consequences. It's also about becoming a sought-after personal brand that makes people happy, successful and remarkable. And, in the spirit of full disclosure, it's also about being attractive to others so they want to be around me.

The play zone is where we find fun. It's who we become at a party when we've unleashed our inner joker, lover or raconteur. It's us at our charismatic, ebullient best.

But the play zone can become the danger zone when we risk becoming inappropriate, wasteful, superficial and exaggerated. Even when we're playing, we need to apply adult supervision – especially in the workplace where one wayward moment can be disastrous.

So the play zone requires both hyper vigilance and bold abandon. We need to be able to let ourselves go, but retain a long leash. It's dancing on the edge of the precipice. That's where the pleasure is most intense. It's also where you can fall down a steep curve.

It's all about controlled exuberance channelled in ways that maximize your joie de vivre without jeopardizing it. So pay attention to the moments of shame, guilt or embarrassment. Either they require an immediate end to your action or an emotional override to neutralize your faulty conditioning.

For example, if I am drunk and boorish at a party, I should feel shame and embarrassment and leave immediately. On the other hand, if I try something new and fail or experience rejection by a prospect or encounter disagreement by fully expressing my opinions at a meeting, I should get over any feelings of shame, discomfort or embarrassment.

How do we know when we've crossed the line? How do we know what the appropriate threshold is for us? How do we condition ourselves to do what we need to do when we need to do it? The answer is in the acronym JADE – judgment, awareness, discretion, experience.

Judgment comes from maturity. It's the ability to see the consequences of your actions in advance.

Awareness is a sense of yourself interacting with your environment. It's the acumen to know what can be said or done under the circumstances.

Discretion is the quality of behaving or speaking in a way to avoid causing offense or revealing private information. It's the signal you can be trusted in all circumstances.

Experience comes with time and practice. It can't be taught in a classroom or be derived from hearsay. It is the result of "being there" over and over again. It's also the dividend you accrue because you're willing to make mistakes on your way to becoming a champion.

The play zone needs to be always present in every person and every organization. There is no life, innovation or imagination without mirth. Laughter is the sound ideas make when they're being born. The greatest places to work are places where people come to smile. They're free to be their best and inspired to help their peers be even better.

It's all about chemistry – the complex emotional and psychological interaction between you and the people around you. The chemistry of happiness is palpable. It's a sparkling energy encouraging everyone to be more and give more because they want to, not because they have to.

Winston Churchill said, "I like a man who grins while he fights." Sometimes, we need to see the funny side of things that are not funny so we can help others grin while they fight. I'm often called into companies during the crisis moments. I've found humour gives people perspective and distance from the problem. If you can make people laugh in the face of threat, you give them the confidence to take it on.

People often ask me why I smile during a serious briefing session detailing the myriad problems facing my client. I reply I'm excited by the scope and novelty of the problems. I also share I'm happy to be employed and wouldn't be if they didn't have these problems. That's when everyone smiles and we can explore solutions in the spirit of positivity and possibility.

There is no purely bad emotional space, only too much time spent there.

Look at the following 60 primary emotions and ask yourself how often you experience them. It's possible to experience multiple emotions at the same time. For the first thirty emotions, give yourself a score of +3 for Often, +2 for Sometimes, +1 for Rarely and 0 for Never. For the second thirty emotions, give yourself -3 for Often, -2 for Sometimes, -1 for Rarely and 0 for Never. Calculate your cumulative score in the final column:

POSITIVE

	Often	Sometimes	Rarely	Never	Running-total
	+3	+2	+1	0	
1. Happy	_____	_____	_____	_____	_______
2. Satisfied	_____	_____	_____	_____	_______
3. Love	_____	_____	_____	_____	_______
4. Pleasure	_____	_____	_____	_____	_______
5. Optimistic	_____	_____	_____	_____	_______
6. Connected	_____	_____	_____	_____	_______
7. Interested	_____	_____	_____	_____	_______
8. Accepted	_____	_____	_____	_____	_______
9. Loyal	_____	_____	_____	_____	_______
10. Trust	_____	_____	_____	_____	_______
11. Respect	_____	_____	_____	_____	_______

POSITIVE

	Often	Sometimes	Rarely	Never	Running-total
	+3	+2	+1	0	
12. Safe	____	____	____	____	______
13. Familiarity	____	____	____	____	______
14. Gratitude	____	____	____	____	______
15. Relaxed	____	____	____	____	______
16. Comforted	____	____	____	____	______
17. Compassion	____	____	____	____	______
18. Blessed	____	____	____	____	______
19. Playful	____	____	____	____	______
20. Romantic	____	____	____	____	______
21. Amused	____	____	____	____	______
22. Entertained	____	____	____	____	______
23. Amazed	____	____	____	____	______
24. Fascinated	____	____	____	____	______
25. Excited	____	____	____	____	______
26. Turned on	____	____	____	____	______
27. Alert	____	____	____	____	______
28. Inspired	____	____	____	____	______
29. Strong	____	____	____	____	______
30. Courageous	____	____	____	____	______

NEGATIVE

	Often	Sometimes	Rarely	Never	Running-total
	-3	-2	-1	0	
31. Isolated	____	____	____	____	______
32. Shocked	____	____	____	____	______
33. Aggressive	____	____	____	____	______
34. Impatient	____	____	____	____	______
35. Bored	____	____	____	____	______
36. Tired	____	____	____	____	______
37. Sad	____	____	____	____	______
38. Disappointed	____	____	____	____	______
39. Distracted	____	____	____	____	______
40. Unappreciated	____	____	____	____	______
41. Excluded	____	____	____	____	______
42. Unbalanced	____	____	____	____	______
43. Confused	____	____	____	____	______
44. Helpless	____	____	____	____	______
45. Shame	____	____	____	____	______
46. Unlucky	____	____	____	____	______
47. Intimidated	____	____	____	____	______
48. Embarrassed	____	____	____	____	______
49. Upset	____	____	____	____	______

NEGATIVE

	Often	Sometimes	Rarely	Never	Running-total
	-3	-2	-1	0	
50. Worried	____	____	____	____	________
51. Disturbed	____	____	____	____	________
52. Jealous	____	____	____	____	________
53. Irritated	____	____	____	____	________
54. Offended	____	____	____	____	________
55. Anger	____	____	____	____	________
56. Hate	____	____	____	____	________
57. Frustrated	____	____	____	____	________
58. Disgusted	____	____	____	____	________
59. Pessimistic	____	____	____	____	________
60. Desperate	____	____	____	____	________

If you scored above 60, you are exceptionally positive. If you scored between 30 and 60, you are solidly positive. If you scored between 0 and 30, you are healthy and you have an opportunity to dial up your positivity through the techniques in this book.

No emotion is bad in itself. Every emotion is essential because, although we think we know what the emotion represents, it's only the tip of the iceberg. For example, when we say we're "scared," we think it's in response to a specific event, person or situation. But under the conscious surface, there's a kaleidoscope of happenings throughout the body from blood flow and chemicals to breathing and thought processes to actions. It's the totality of the emotion's impact on every aspect of our mind and body that builds our capacity to cope.

So go through each emotion. Don't resist your emotional tides. But also don't be swept away by them. If we're conscious to the specific emotion we're experiencing and how we're responding to it, we can influence its impact both on us and on others. We're all part of each other's emotional fields. Whatever you're feeling, others in your orbit will feel it as well.

If you are only excited and never adversely affected by your surroundings, you may be unhealthy because health equals balance. Health isn't only correlated with positive emotions. Health is comprised of opposites – happiness, excitement, confidence, disappointment, fatigue, confusion and pain. It takes one kind of emotion to illuminate its opposite.

So as you review your experience of the emotions I listed for you, be alert to the "always" or "never." Power is about flow. You can't experience one pole without experiencing its polar opposite. For example, a vacation without work to go back to is hell. It loses its reason for being. All play and no work will diminish and destroy our productive capacity. All work and no play will burn us out. Relaxation and stress go together like a needle and thread.

Then look at your "often" and "rarely." If you're bored and tired more often than interested and excited, it could spell trouble. Yet we shouldn't be afraid of the dark emotional spaces. Night always follows day. Shadows are always generated by sunlight. People fear disappointment. Or they never want to feel cheated. Or hate to hate. Or try to avoid disgust or dissatisfaction. So they ration their hope or trust or optimism or love. We have to spend time in the dark, just not too much time.

Disappointment, frustration or desperation are not diseases. They're incentives to act. So are familiarity, safety and pleasure. We need the peace of mind that "home" brings, but we also need the adrenalin, dopamine and endorphins that come with breaking out of our comfort zones. It's a physiological need for stimulation and interest that becomes milder over time. Teenagers feel it most intensely. Then it begins to dissipate. That's why the older we get, the more we need to challenge and stretch ourselves.

If you want to get it, you have to get out. Literally. There is a direct correlation between creativity and talking to many different people. When we travel to far-off places, we come back with different points of view. Foreign experiences enrich our local content.

We can choose to break out of our mental habits. Who we read and who we listen to can reshape our mental landscapes.

We can also use different words. By simply changing our language, we can change our experience of the world. Listen to young people talk and you'll hear the outrageous language of extremes, words like - wicked, shocking, sick, awesome, intense – which all express good experiences. Think about the words we're using in this book. They've been chosen to rock you out of your rut in a way that motivates you into powerful action.

My favourite word is "fascinating." It means being spellbound, compelled or magnetized by something or someone.

It's when I'm at my best. The opposite of fascinating for me is frustrating. That's when I'm at my worst because I don't have the resources or energy to resolve problems or connect with people. Yet fascination is also close to "shock." This is when I'm tipped into upset or worry. But even shock is a positive emotion for me. It's when I am shaken out of my complacency and knocked off balance. It prepares me for learning. It leads to amazement and astonishment. It heightens my alertness and sensitivity to my environment.

You can't be great if you're in a small world. You need to inhabit the biggest world that is open to you. Our area of knowledge is directly proportional to the frontier of the unknown we choose to explore. The more we know, the more we realize we don't know. And the more inspired we become to find out more. The more questions we ask, the more motivated we become to ask more. The only difference between inspired and overwhelmed is the personal choice we make.

Delight in the everyday.

We cannot change our DNA, but we can change our direction. A tiny shift can open up a whole new view. If there is one thing I've learned from studying over a million people, it's this: we can consciously choose what to pay attention to. Next we can decide to take action. We can sustain our focus. We can develop new habits. And then we can help others do the same.

Great happiness doesn't come from great events; it comes from great appreciation of the small things. By definition, great events are few and far between. But it's the everyday events that ultimately determine the quality of our lives.

Happiness is a function of our ability to derive maximum pleasure from the things we do most often. In my case, it's conversation. I love to talk, I love to listen and I love to distil and share my learning. That's why I'm writing this book. It's one long conversation with you I've captured in writing.

The secret to feeling like a champion is to "delight in the everyday." Nothing in life has any meaning except the meaning we give it. We need to consciously override our prior programming that discounts the magic of our present reality or inflates the fear of forthcoming challenges.

Today you will have so many opportunities to be upset, stressed or annoyed. Today you will be confronted by ignorance, indifference or insolence. Today you will experience multiple reversals, mistakes or frustrations. Between now and bedtime, you will take a journey of a thousand cuts that could bleed you out and suck you dry.

Yet today you will be granted your daily miracles. You will smile, laugh or play with a friend. You will work, build or create something amazing with a colleague. You'll read, learn or hear about a breakthrough from an unexpected source. You'll eat or drink something delicious. You'll be warmed, enthused or inspired by someone remarkable.

All of this will happen a hundred times today. And tomorrow. And the day after. Just like yesterday and the days before that. These are the little things building our lives or breaking them down. Where you are today is a direct result of how you handle the little things.

Here's a big question: what about the big things? Birth, death, marriage, divorce, buying a house, starting a business, closing a big deal, getting promoted, getting sick, getting well, saving a life, winning the lottery?

Maybe all these things are big. But they're no bigger than the conversation I'm having with you right now. They're no bigger than the lunch I have planned with a great friend. Or the presentation I'm giving this afternoon or family dinner I have planned for this evening. The so-called big things may happen once a year, decade or lifetime. They may even happen once a month. But the so-called little things happen every day, maybe even every hour. Hey, maybe they even happen every minute or every second. Like, for example, breathing.

If you can't do the little things right, you'll never get the big things right. Revel in the day. Seize the seconds to achieve firsts. Don't hang back when you need to step forward. You don't have to be an extrovert but don't let your natural reserve get in the way of opportunity.

Take it on.

Take on the thing that scares you. Take on the person who scares you. Take on the scary challenge.

Anyone who tells you they're fearless is being disingenuous. The future is bright, bold and full of bogeymen. If you're playing a big game for a big prize, it's going to be hard. The competition is going to be amazing. The clients are going to be incredibly demanding. The standards are going to be unreasonably high. It's going to take everything you have and then some.

I've been helping clients become champions for 23 years. I have worked with over a million people in 43 countries. But in the last year, I've witnessed a whole new level of intensity. Extreme is the new normal. Volatility is the new stability. Low growth is the new high-opportunity zone.

Success takes experience and courage in equal measure. Courage without experience equals naïveté.

There is no short cut to wisdom. Wisdom is the capacity to use accumulated knowledge, understanding, common sense and enlightenment to create new solutions to new problems. The magic ingredient is time. Patience is a virtue when it's applied in the right measure. We need to watch, listen, learn, act and improve every day in every way.

As Steve Jobs said, "Creativity is just connecting things. When you ask creative people how they did something, they feel a little guilty because they didn't really do it, they just saw something. It seemed obvious to them after a while. That's because they were able to connect experiences they've had and synthesize new things."

The moral of the story is whether you're Steve Jobs or Mike Lipkin or Joanne Citizen, when you take on the thing that scares you, fear turns into a resource. You mobilize yourself into action. You strengthen your champion muscles. You mend your broken wings and fly.

That's right. The longer you fly, the greater the chance your wings have been broken. We've all flown into headwinds. We've hit walls. We've had great falls and learned to put ourselves back together again. That's what makes us stronger. Paul McCartney gets it right when he sings:

> Blackbird singing in the dead of night

Take these broken wings and learn to fly

All your life

You were only waiting for this moment to arise

Blackbird singing in the dead of night

Take these sunken eyes and learn to see

All your life

You were only waiting for this moment to be free

Blackbird fly blackbird fly

Into the light of the dark black night.

"Into the light of the dark black night." That line was written in June 1968 but it's more relevant today than ever before. We're hurtling into the future at warp speed. We're all making it up as we go along. We're all actors learning our roles and mastering them at the same time.

Jeff Daniels, the celebrated actor, recently appeared on Broadway in the play Blackbird with Michelle Williams. It's a soul scorcher of a story about a relationship between an older man and a younger woman. It was also the second time that Daniels played this part. Here's how he described his challenge:

"Every actor knows that you can't run from the ones that scare you. It's not the acting of the character nor is it the dark imagination it takes to put yourself through all of his guilt and shame. To truly become someone else, you have to hear him in your head, thinking, justifying, defending, wanting, needing, desiring. The more I looked back at the first production, the more I saw what I hadn't done, where I hadn't gone. I'd pulled up short, found ways around what was necessary."

That's the power of experience. You look back on what you could have done so you can look forward to what you can do. The secret is to run towards the things that scare you so you can take on even bigger dragons.

What you don't face will haunt you until you do. So take it on. But don't take it on alone. Jeff Daniels needs Michelle Williams. I need my partners, clients and friends. I trust them to be there with me when I take it on. Who do you trust and who can trust you to help them take it on?

Trust first. Trust fast. Trust strong.

Of all the things I've shared with you in this book, this could be the most important: Trust first. Trust fast. Trust strong. Trust others until they give you a reason not to. Tell them you trust them. Tell them why you trust them. Hold them accountable to your trust. Forgive them when they fall short the first time. Give them a second chance. If it happens a third time, walk away.

I am who I am because of all the people I trust. Every day I'm trusting more people with the things that matter most to me. And every day they make me trust them more. I choose my allies carefully and they almost never let me down. When things go south, it's usually my fault anyway.

In summary, based on my research with over a million people around the world, I believe that the champions of the future will share five emotions in common.

FIRST, CHAMPIONS WILL BE COURAGEOUS

Courage is the most important emotion because it's the one from which all others spring. Just like everyone else, champions feel the fear. But they'll use it to bring out their best. The great writer Margaret Atwood said, "Heroes need monsters to establish their heroic credentials. You need something scary to overcome."

So champions will be both cautious and curious. They will be comfortable being uncomfortable. They'll worry about the future but convert their worry into anticipatory action. For example, I'm worried about 2017 because 2017 is going to be the most challenging year of all time. I'm going to have to transform myself faster than my environment, which is changing at warp speed. That's why I'm creating this book. It's my way of anticipating what I need to do to win. By communicating my insights with you, I'm empowering you to be successful. I know you'll pay it forward and I'll be paid back very well. What anticipatory action can you take to be a champion in 2017?

SECOND, CHAMPIONS WILL BE EXCITED

They will interpret their environment in ways that make them enthusiastic, eager and energetic. Where others see blocks and barriers, they'll see gaps and openings. They relish their lives and all the possibilities. They're always fascinated by what's in front of them. As Helen Keller said, "Life is a daring adventure."

Steve Gupta, a leading property developer in Toronto, came to Canada 40 years ago but still thinks of himself as a "New Canadian." He still looks at his adopted country through the eyes of someone who has just arrived. He's always excited. That's why he sees so much more than his counterparts. What could you see if you looked at today through new lenses?

J.K. Rowling was a struggling single mother before she wrote the first Harry Potter book. She said, "Harry Potter gave me back self respect. Harry gave me a job to do that I loved more than anything else." What job could you love more than anything else?

THIRD, CHAMPIONS WILL BE ENGAGED

They're all in. They're committed to all their communities. They step up. They know they're only as good as how good they make others. Champions are volunteers – they don't do what they do because they have to. They do it because they want to. They find reasons to reach out, not excuses to hold back. They err on the side of action. They would rather try something than do nothing.

There is a direct correlation between their commitment to the cause and their personal happiness: engagement equals happiness. The opposite of happiness isn't sadness, it's isolation. Apathy is not an option. If you lose yourself in the service of others, you'll find exactly what you're looking for.

FOURTH, CHAMPIONS WILL BE AT EASE

Champions find the quiet place in the eye of the paradox. Despite the stress and strain, they radiate wellbeing. Their minds are relaxed. That's why you feel relaxed when you're around them. They know when to move and when to be still. You're attracted to them because they make you feel cool, calm and collected. Champions become your go-to people. I'm privileged to have many champions in my life. They make it seem easy especially when it's hard. But they work very hard to make it seem easy.

Champions are self-aware. They understand their impact on others so they manage their impact on themselves. There was a reason Muhammad Ali said, "I am the greatest." A reason why Martin Luther King said, "I have a dream." A reason Steve Jobs said, "We want to make the best products for people." They say great things to themselves so they can say great things to others.

FIFTH, CHAMPIONS WILL BE GENEROUS

Champions understand true power is reciprocal. They more they give, the more valuable they become. Champions give especially when it's inconvenient or difficult. They're motivated by the sheer pleasure of contribution but they also harvest its rewards. They're the ones others respond to first. If all you do as a result of this book is give as much as you can to as many people as you can today, my work will be worthwhile.

When you give, you open up the flow from you and towards you. I have always regretted giving less. I have never regretted giving more. Sharing magnifies success. Jamil Zaki, an assistant professor of psychology at Stanford University, wrote in The New York Times (December 6, 2015), "Generosity not only makes givers feel good, but reduces their stress level. Students who acted kindly experienced lower levels of stress and anxiety than their less generous peers. But this was true only to the extent that people feel empathy while helping others." In other words, if you really care about the people you're helping, you multiply the beneficial impact of your generosity on yourself. Makes you think, doesn't it?

So make courage, excitement, engagement, ease and generosity part of your emotional portfolio in 2017. Build them one thought, one action, one contribution at a time. Switch off your auto-pilot. Turn on your intentional awareness. Develop your antennae. Listen for feedback. Adapt as you go along. Try on new approaches.

And, above all, be guided by this question: Am I a joy to be around? Count every moment because every moment counts.

By now, you identify as a champion. You dream like a champion. You plan like a champion. You feel like a champion. Congratulations. You've made it to the starting line. You're ready to win. Now it's time to get on the field. It's time to play like a champion. As the great Chinese general, Sun Tzu, said in 500BC, "Victorious warriors win first, then go to war while defeated warriors go to war first, then seek to win."

5

"PLAY LIKE A CHAMPION TODAY"

TRUE CHAMPIONS ARE AUDACIOUS (AWE-DAY-SHUS)

BE RESILIENT - THE STARS ALIGN FOR THOSE WHO FIGHT THE GOOD FIGHT AND STAY THE COURSE

BE A CATALYST THROUGH COLLABORATION – MULTIPLY OTHERS' POWER SO THEY CAN MAGNIFY YOURS

ACT YOUR ROLE

REGENERATE YOURSELF

"PLAY LIKE A CHAMPION TODAY"

It's just a simple wooden sign, painted gold and blue and mounted on a cream-coloored brick wall at the foot of a stairwell. Yet the "Play Like a Champion Today" sign, found outside Notre Dame's locker room, is so much more.

The slogan "Play Like a Champion Today" is so synonymous with the university you can be excused for believing Father Edward Sorin, the school's founder, received it as a divine revelation in 1842.

While the exact origin of the slogan is unknown, the sign currently hanging in Notre Dame Stadium came courtesy of former coach Lou Holtz. "I read a lot of books about the history of Notre Dame and its football program," Holtz explains. "I forget which book I was looking at - it had an old picture in it that showed the slogan 'Play Like a Champion Today.' I said, 'That is really appropriate; it used to be at Notre Dame and we needed to use it again.' So, I had that sign made up."

Soon, the tradition of hitting the sign before every game developed. Holtz even used a copy of the sign when travelling to road contests to help motivate the team.

You can't play like a champion yesterday. You can't even play like a champion tomorrow. You can only play like a champion this day. This moment. So here I am on Monday, February 15, 2016, playing like a champion. I'm writing with all the intensity I can muster. I'm swinging for the fences and hitting my words out the park. I can hear the audience in my head. I can see your smile in my mind. I can feel the impending impact in my heart. Bring it on, baby!

The great coach and co-founder of the NFL George Halas said, "No one who ever gave his best, regretted it." You can't always play at your best. You're a human not a machine. Some days are going to be easier on you than others. But you can always give your best. Champions reach the point where that's the only way they know how to play. They don't always get the results they want, but they always leave it all on the field.

It's "play like a champion," not "work like a champion."

Joy is the fuel on which champions run. The uncommon denominator uniting them is their unbridled enthusiasm for their mission. They love what they do and it shows. Some may seize every opportunity to evangelize their purpose and others may prefer to whisper. But all of them radiate their infinite fascination with their craft.

If you're not playing, it's hard work. And hard work is tiring. Eventually, it exhausts you no matter how enduring you are. Play, on the other hand, is self-renewing. After 23 years of enabling people to become champions, I'm still enchanted by the childlike glee that lights up champions even after decades in their role. It's a rare and beautiful thing to be with someone whose passion for the grind continually sharpens their edge.

Earlier I mentioned DHL Express, one of the world's leading express logistics companies. Ken Allen took over as CEO of the global business in 2009 during the depth of the global financial meltdown. At the same time, the company was hemorrhaging money in the U.S. where it was ill equipped to compete domestically with industry champions like UPS and FedEx. Within two years he had stabilized the business. Within four years, he had grown earnings before interest and tax to one billion Euros. Today, DHL Express is a best-in-class performer in market share, employer of choice and profitability. Allen has become known as the "Singing CEO" because of his love for classic pop music. He also stages annual "DHL's Got Talent" shows where every country in the DHL network competes for prizes and the right to perform in front of the global management board. Here's how he describes his strategy:

> "We have introduced what we would call 'incremental innovation' – small but significant changes to the way we work that help us to communicate our strategy to frontline employees and engage them. For example, we make active use of singing (yes, that's right, singing), using popular music to translate complex strategic focus areas into a language everyone can understand. The 1960s Ashford and Simpson classic Ain't No Mountain High Enough, for example, is used to communicate the 'can do' values that we want our employees to apply in their daily work. We've found that it's much more effective than a spreadsheet or flow chart in getting emotional buy-in from a courier or warehouse worker. We have also institutionalized small gestures of appreciation – it could be a pizza, a Manchester United T-shirt or simply a personalized thank you from your manager or supervisor – through regular Appreciation Weeks. A small gesture might not mean so much to someone sitting at headquarters on a management salary, but it can mean the world to a courier who's navigating his way heroically but inconspicuously across the Kazakh steppe every day to deliver packages to an oil field on the Caspian Sea."

If you currently love what you do, you're definitely nodding your head in agreement with these words. But what if you don't find joy in your work? Your choice is either to find work that thrills you or find reasons to be thrilled by your work. You can either change the situation or change your attitude towards your situation.

The alternative is to be a champion in areas outside of your work. Then your work funds your real calling. And that's just fine - on one condition: your lack of passion cannot interfere with other people's commitment to the cause.

Recently I coached a 50-something leader who had lost her love for her company. She still enjoyed her industry but was resentful she was working so hard to make other people rich. She wasn't playing full out in meetings. She wasn't being creative. She wasn't stretching to help her colleagues win. She was doing "just enough" to pay her way. But she was miserable and her ambivalence was being noticed. Together, we decided she could stay with the company and find a way to give her heart and soul or she could strike out on her own and start a new company. In the meantime, at least she knew she had a choice. She was free to pilot her own course forward. As I write these words, she is still with her company and she is "playing like a champion."

Luck isn't a lottery. It's a way of being. It's created from the inside out, not the outside in.

If you read this book and hand me a fabulous opportunity to motivate thousands of people, I will be lucky. But the opportunity would never have happened without this book. We create our own luck by ensuring we seize our fair share of good fortune. Every word in this book is a magnet to the chances that are rightfully mine. I don't want any of them to get away.

Writing this book is a "marquee action." It's the most compelling declaration I can make about my candidacy for your time, attention and money. But it's complemented by an array of other everyday activities designed to attract the right kind of attention and follow-through. I know if I play the odds, the odds will turn in my favour.

What actions are you taking that will magnetize your chances to you? Seriously, how are you expressing your right to be lucky? What's your exclamation of intent? Can anybody even hear you? Would anybody vote for you based on your current activities?

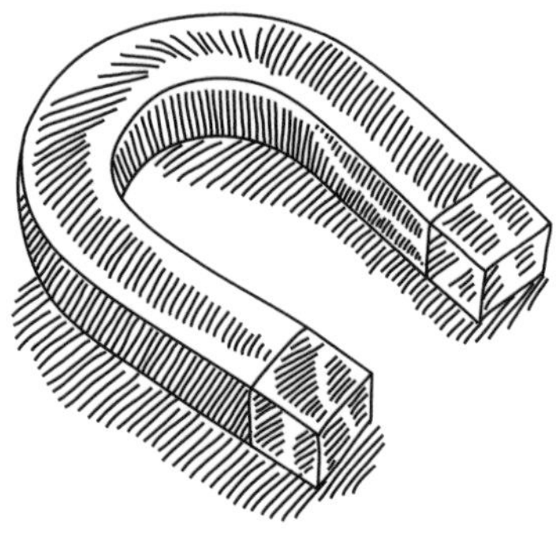

No one wakes up and says, "Today, I'm going to be bored, disengaged and anxious at work." But it happens and it's a slow moving tragedy. Boredom is the side effect of "drift." That's when we get sucked into sidebars and dominated by "administrivia." The paperwork becomes the work even though there's very little paper any more. What makes us great is cannibalized by what makes us small. Petty issues dry up our creative juices and make us hard and cynical.

Somewhere inside everyone the magic is hibernating in anticipation of the right time. If you're reading this, your time is now. So what will it take to unleash your unique and extraordinary power? What kind of signal are you waiting for? If not now, then when?

Here's the new irony: human beings are living longer but the life of things they crave is becoming shorter. The winners last longer by moving faster in areas that count. They also know when to slow down or stop and change direction. In the new parlance, it's called "pivoting" – changing strategy and focus in pursuit of the same goals.

Practice is the most important word in the vocabulary of champions.

Practice is defined by the Random House Dictionary as "repeated performance or systematic exercise for the purpose of acquiring skill or proficiency; condition arrived at by experience or exercise; the action or process of performing or doing something."

The key words are: repeated, systematic exercise, purpose, condition, action, process, doing. Practice is an active verb but it's also a state of being. We refer to a professional's practice. That's literally where he works but it's also something he has built through repeated actions over time.

It's easier to act your way into a way of thinking than think your way into a way of acting. Read that statement again. We learn by doing. We get ready to do something by doing it before we're ready. That's how we become ready. On the other hand, just sitting and thinking by yourself in a dark room may prepare you for nothing more than more inertia.

When we discipline our practice and practice our discipline, we increase our capacity to achieve remarkable results. We develop an operating rhythm that builds our momentum. To others it seems like we're on a roll. We appear both lucky and smart. The truth is luck is a matter of chance. That means it is distributed equally across everyone. We've studied millions of people in tens of countries. The difference between lucky and unlucky is the bias towards action or non-action. It's not more luck that makes the difference; it's the return that one generates on luck – ROL (Return On Luck). The greater the practice, the greater the luck.

In his book, The Way of the Fight, the renowned martial artist Georges St-Pierre says, "One of the lessons I learnt in all those years of practicing karate is that progress only comes in small, incremental portions. Nobody becomes great overnight. Nobody crams information if he wants to be able to use it over the long term. I have a belief that all human greatness is founded on routine, that truly great human behaviour is impossible without this central part of your life being set up and governed by routine. You don't get better on the days when you feel like going. You get better on the days when you don't want to go, but you go anyway. If you can overcome the negative energy coming from your tired body or unmotivated mind, you will grow and become better. Growth is a long term game and the crappy days are more important."

Playing like a champion means delivering excellence on demand. It means your variance in performance is so small it's almost indiscernible to the people depending on you to be excellent. It's about repeatability, but it's also about trusting yourself to replicate your best performance every time you perform.

When I get in front of a highly discerning audience, I have to uplift and delight them. It's irrelevant what mood or state I'm in. The only thing that counts is their experience. If I just "meet expectations," I've failed. I have to blow away their preconceptions and imbue them with a plethora of possibilities. My safety net is my belief in my ability to play preeminently every time, even when I don't. The second that I second-guess myself, I'm lost. Practice enables the right actions, but it also enables the right beliefs.

In the world of champions, many wrongs make it right.

If you break the law, that's wrong. If you fail to understand the laws of physics or mathematics, you'll come up with the wrong answer. If you don't understand someone's language, you'll talk to her in the wrong language. If you ignore the law of gravity, you'll pay gravely for being wrong. That kind of wrong is real. It's definitive and measurable. There's a clear right way and a wrong way.

In the world of champions, however, right is never rigid. It's relative. It's transient and transforming. Wrong can be right because it's pursuing the next expression of *right now.*

Whoever said, "get it right first time" only got it half right. *Right* is an ambiguous notion. It could be conformance with existing standards or free from mistakes or flaws. In these cases, you can get it right first time. Or, right could mean the best expression of the genre or ideal execution of the product or service. In these cases, right is iterative. Each version builds on the previous one to enhance its performance on the way to perfect.

Right is often the result of taking missteps in the right direction. By looking in all the wrong places, we find things we didn't expect to see. Each discovery is a deposit on our perspective. Sometimes it's pretty and sometimes it's not. What matters is the practice of searching for our desired outcome and creating the space for others to do so as well.

Winners will always lose more than losers because they are trying more things. As Adam Grant wrote in the March 2016 issue of the Harvard Business Review, "Being prolific actually increases originality because sheer volume improves your chances of finding novel solutions. Even the most eminent innovators do their most original work when they're also cranking out scores of less brilliant ideas. The more darts you throw, the better your odds of hitting a bull's eye."

James Dyson, the founder and CEO of Dyson, the highly innovative manufacturer of vacuum cleaners, hair dryers, fans and heaters states, "Failure is just part of the process. It took me 15 years and 5127 attempts to develop the first bagless cyclonic vacuum. I won't lie – it was frustrating and aggravating, but it was also invigorating and exciting. What matters about failure is that you learn from it. Perhaps the biggest thing that holds inventors back might be our impatience. It's important to teach people that if you fail once, you're one step closer to success. It's failure that drives invention forward."

One of my favourite activities out of Africa was leaving behind the trappings of city life and going into a game park. As a speaker, I would often participate in corporate offsites held in these remarkable locations. On rare occasions, we would witness a pride of lions catching and feasting on their prey. It always struck me how violent it was. While the lions executed a practice refined over many hunts, there was no instant "killer blow." It would take lion after lion to leap onto the prey and try pull it down. The buffalo or the zebra or the wildebeest would fight back with horns and hooves. Often, it would escape. And even when the lions were successful, it was a battle of attrition. The prey would be worn down by multiple assaults until it succumbed to the fatal bite. It was bloody and exhausting for hunter and prey alike.

Every time the lions set out to hunt, they expected a titanic battle with their prey. Even though they are masters of their craft, they don't expect it to get any easier. However, they expect to win because they need to eat.

Being a champion becomes more difficult as you grow old. But that's what I'm signing up for. Like the lions, I want to eat and I want to eat well. It's in the leaping that the solutions appear. But unlike the lions, all the violence is happening on the inside as I try to kill whatever is getting in the way of these words. As David Cronenberg the renowned film director said, "Everybody is a mad scientist and life is their lab. We're all trying to experiment to find a way to live, to solve problems, to fend off madness and chaos."

Amazon founder Jeff Bezos said, "It's not an experiment if you know it's going to work." Playing like a champion means playing the game while you change it. It means not knowing how long the game will last or what the end result will be. It also entails being so committed to the game that you'll see it through to the end, because the end of one game is merely the beginning of the next. By definition, the game is never over. There are just time-outs.

The best kind of practice isn't practice. Practice doesn't make perfect. Even perfect practice doesn't make perfect. Playing for real makes us perfect. There's a huge difference between rehearsing and performing. The game-changer is the stress of competition and consequence. I've seen perfect rehearsals devolve into debacles because people couldn't handle the tension of real-time competition. Even the air seems different when the whistle blows for the actual game.

Like me, you're probably not a professional athlete. That means you don't have to wait for the actual game to earn your game-time. You can turn every situation into the game by treating every activity like it's a defining activity. No casual moments allowed. Every move disciplines your mind to perform preeminently under pressure. For example, I treat every conversation with every client like it's a marquee presentation. I consciously invest all my energy and presence into every word. I know that kind of awareness produces the kind of impact that wins me the opportunity. It also becomes a conscious habit. Watch my videos at **www.mikelipkin.com** and you'll see what I mean. Whether you like my style or not, there is no doubting my conviction or intensity. Every video is a showcase of my talent to potential clients. It's the work and the work is the message. It has to hit the mark for the people who matter.

In the heat of the game, anything that gets in the way of flow will damage your impact. The fundamentals should be second nature, enabling you to focus on the nuances that brand you as a maestro – a master of your art. In my case, it's being able to share powerful inspirational messages fluently and entertainingly for up to eight hours at a time. What is it in your case? And if I saw you perform, would I say to myself, "she's the best I've seen?"

The performance paradox is you can't be a maestro if you're trying too hard to be a maestro. If you're too attached to looking good, you'll end up looking bad. Your vanity will get in the way of your authenticity. You'll become the focus of your delivery, not the people you're serving.

The core question is not, "What if I don't perform well?" It's "How can I amaze my clients with so much value they're captivated by the experience?" If you ask the right questions, you'll find the right answers, but only if you're practiced enough.

Embrace embarrassment.

Embarrassment is the flip side to differentiation. Being special means putting yourself in a space where others aren't prepared to go. That statement alone sets you apart from the pack. It's delicious when it works and can feel ugly when it doesn't. Success is the premium we earn for risking embarrassment.

Embarrassment is really just acute self-consciousness. It's a feeling of foolishness because of something you've said or done. But here's the thing: most the time, our feelings of foolishness are out of proportion to how other people perceive our words or actions. In fact, our actions could have elicited extremely positive perceptions. What you may regard as stupidity, naïveté or awkwardness, other may consider openness, vulnerability or authenticity.

In my seminars, people frequently approach me to share their embarrassment because they've misinterpreted a colleagues' response to something they said. The truth is hardly anyone was even paying attention or, in the context of the overall event, it didn't even register in their minds. If you knew how little time others spend thinking about you, you wouldn't worry what they think of you.

To quote Martin Luther King, "The arc of the moral universe is long, but it bends towards justice." There will be moments when you do the right thing without getting the right results. There are always multiple variables at play. Sometimes, it's entirely subjective – other people don't like what you've said or they prefer another person's approach. Sometimes, timing is not on your side. And sometimes, you acted like you were unsure of yourself and others shared your doubt. Over time, however, tenacity pays off. It can take years to become an overnight success.

THE FIVE PLAYS OF A CHAMPION

In the end, the only thing that matters is results. As Dani Reiss the CEO of Canada Goose says, "Magic is hard work but not everyone who works hard creates magic." Like you, I know a lot of people who work hard but produce mediocre results. They may see themselves as champions, dream like champions, plan like champions and even feel like champions. But they lack the vital ingredients required to play like champions.

I met many of these people recently on Beale Street in Memphis, Tennessee. Beale Street is a 1.8-mile strip packed with live music clubs and blues bars. The musicians are supremely talented. To my appreciative ears, they sounded just as good as the iconic artists whose music they were playing. And yet they were making only modest incomes. The problem is they weren't the composers of their own music. They were playing someone else's songs. Even though they were world class, they were still imitating the true champions.

The true champions achieve magic results through five plays:

1. True champions are audacious (awe-day-shus).
2. Be resilient - the stars align for those who fight the good fight and stay the course.
3. Be a catalyst through collaboration – multiply others' power so they can magnify yours.
4. Act your role.
5. Regenerate yourself.

TRUE CHAMPIONS ARE AUDACIOUS (AWE-DAY-SHUS)

"To be a prolific outside shooter in the NBA requires an almost comical amount of optimism. A player has to accept that more than half of his shots will miss but has to retain the confidence to thrust the ball towards the rim every time he has the chance." Benjamin Hoffman, (The New York Times, November 16, 2014)

Say "audacious" aloud. Say it like you mean it. Say it again. Think about the way your mouth moves when you articulate the word. Even if you didn't know what it meant, just saying it is awe-inspiring.

If you're audacious, it means that you are willing to take surprisingly bold risks. You show an irreverent lack of respect for the status quo. You're extremely original. You're not inhibited by others' opinions or constrained by prior ideas. Does that describe you? When was the last time that you took a surprisingly bold risk? How often are you inhibited by others' opinions or constrained by prior ideas? How can you demonstrate your audaciousness in your chosen arena?

Champions are driven to reinvent the game. No matter how high they've climbed, they always have something to prove. They open up the space for breakthroughs to occur. They dare to go where others fear to tread. They're not fearless and they're not reckless. They simply understand they have to be audacious if they want to be a champion. There is no other path to greatness. Either they take the bull by the horns or the bull takes them.

Look around you right now. Everything you're wearing, using, eating, reading or watching is the result of someone being audacious enough to take surprisingly bold risks. Someone made a big bet they could do something better than anyone had ever done it before and proved themselves right.

When I came to North America in 2001, I aspired to be a world-class motivational speaker. This is the only continent in the world where the FAIM industry (fulfilment, ambition, inspiration and motivation) is an integral part of the business culture. It isn't fantasy or just nice-to-have. It's a fundamental necessity. It's what enables the future to break from the past. In this culture, it doesn't matter where you come from. What matters is where you're going. Everything is predicated on being able to first imagine then execute new solutions to new problems.

My first year in Toronto was scary. Although I had the support of my partners at Environics, I struggled to establish my credentials as a coach who understood the finer points of North American culture. I was an "African in Canada" presuming to know what was best for Americans and Canadians.

That's when I discovered a uniquely American word that expresses the essence of being audacious – **gumption**. Just saying it gives me impetus. Gumption is a blend of courage, resourcefulness, shrewdness, confidence aggressiveness, stick-to-itiveness and spunk. It only exists through action.

I asked myself what it would take to demonstrate gumption. I evaluated how I could demonstrate it. Then I did it – over and over again. Win or lose, I wanted to show the world I had gumption. I shared my motivation with everyone I spoke to. Ironically that message became my strongest selling point. Then, as now, people were feeling overwhelmed and anxious about the future. In a post 9-11 world, people needed to rediscover their gumption. Who better to help them do it than a brand new immigrant just beginning his new incarnation?

I learned when you don't have a safety net, you still have to take the leap. Once you leap the safety net appears. As renowned feminist activist and writer Sonia Johnson said, "It's only when we have nothing else to hold onto that we're willing to try something very audacious and scary." You didn't come this far without your own brand of gumption. Now your challenge is to raise your bets with the cards you have.

Here are three examples of champion gumption that will galvanize you into bold action:

Carli Lloyd

In the 2015 Women's Soccer World Cup Final between the USA and Japan, Carli Lloyd became the first woman to score three goals in a final. What's more, she scored three goals in the first 16 minutes. Her third goal was part genius and part fluke. She took possession of the ball from the halfway line and noticed the Japanese goalkeeper was way off her goal line. So she kicked an arcing shot that eluded the goalkeeper and entered the net just inside the left-hand post. It was one of the most ambitious shots in soccer history. She scored but even if she didn't score, she took the shot. She had the vision, the belief and the skill to do it.

Lloyd sums up her playing philosophy as follows, "Every time I step in between those lines, I'm in the zone. If you get between me and the ball, you might get smashed a couple times. Things happen, plays happen. Nothing dirty. You want to keep it clean. You just want to play hard. Get your jersey dirty, shorts dirty and just have fun out there."

Sarah Blakely

Spanx founder Sara Blakely was getting ready for a party when she realized she didn't have the right undergarment to provide a smooth look under white pants. Armed with scissors and sheer genius, she cut the feet off her control top pantyhose and the Spanx revolution began. With a focus on solving wardrobe woes, the Spanx brand has grown to offer bras, underwear, jeans, pants, active wear and more.

As reported in Forbes (October 21, 2014), in the early days of Spanx, inventor Sara Blakely didn't have the money to hire a patent lawyer, let alone a full team to support her new business. Her office was her Atlanta apartment. Her fulfilment centre was her bathroom, filled with Jiffy envelopes of her product, the now-ubiquitous shapewear that has since made her a billionaire.

So in 2000 when Oprah Winfrey came calling, wanting to add Spanx to her famous "Favorite Things" episode, Blakely had a problem. The Harpo production team wanted to film Blakely, then 27, at a staff meeting in her workplace. She corralled some local friends and faked a workforce for the camera.

That anecdote is typical of Blakely's early years, when she spent nights in the Georgia Tech library researching patent law (she wrote her own patent, with a textbook from Barnes and Noble). She spent weekends driving the five and a half hours to North Carolina, knocking on the doors of hosiery mills, begging them to manufacture her product. "They'd ask who my financial backers were," she said, "I'd say, 'Sara Blakely.'"

The Florida native's hustle paid off when she finagled a meeting at Neiman Marcus' corporate HQ in Dallas. She flew there with a pair of Spanx in her lucky red backpack. Two minutes into her meeting, she could tell she was losing the attention of Neiman Marcus' buyer. She whisked her into the bathroom for a little show and tell, trying on her own product — slimming, shaping footless pantyhose — under a pair of white pants.

Her gumption and willingness to literally put her own ass on the line worked. Neiman Marcus agreed to stock Spanx in seven regional stores. And, still a hustler at heart, Blakely dispatched friends in each of those seven cities to buy pairs of Spanx (she'd mail them cheques for their trouble).

Today, Blakely remains 100 percent owner of Spanx, the company that made her the youngest self-made female billionaire in the world and landed her on the cover of Forbes in 2012. She has never formally advertised, nor has she taken outside investment. The popularity and success of the product has been almost entirely the result of word of mouth and buzz.

"I did not have the most experience in the industry or the most money," Blakely recalled on stage of those first tough years. "But I cared the most."

Blakely epitomizes the ethos of fun as a core ingredient of success. As she says, "I feel like money makes you more of who you already are. If you're an asshole, you become a bigger asshole. If you're nice, you become nicer. Money is fun to make, fun to spend and fun to give away."

Jerry Seinfeld

We all know Jerry Seinfeld as the star of his record-breaking sitcom series and stand up comedian. But with his web series, Comedians in Cars Getting Coffee, he's also a master of the internet.

In Comedians in Cars Getting Coffee, Seinfeld indulges his passion for classic sports cars while engaging celebrity guests in conversations designed to reveal an authentic part of them. His guests have included President Barack Obama, Tina Fey, Sarah Jessica Parker and Amy Schumer. Episodes have been streamed over 100 million times since its debut in 2012. The show is now a core part of Sony's up-start network Crackle, in its bid to become a major player in online content.

According to The New York Times (May 31, 2015) Seinfeld said, "the internet is the least forgiving medium of anything. Even at a nightclub, an audience can't all get up and leave. On the internet they can."

After being told no one would watch online videos more than a couple minutes long, Seinfeld created videos that were over 15 minutes. He said, "The less you know about a field, the better your odds. Dumb boldness is the best way to approach a new challenge." That may just be the best definition of audacity ever written.

Are you a wolf or a dog?

On June 8, 2014, John Coates, a research fellow from Cambridge who traded derivatives for Goldman Sachs, wrote in The New York Times, "When opportunities abound, a potent cocktail of dopamine – a neurotransmitter operating along the pleasure pathways of the brain – and testosterone encourages us to expand our risk taking, a physical transformation that I refer to as 'the hour between dog and wolf'. One opportunity is a brief spike in market volatility, for this presents a chance to make money. But if the volatility rises for a long period, the prolonged uncertainty leads us to subconsciously conclude that we no longer understand what is happening and then cortisol scales back our risk taking. In this way, our risk taking calibrates to the amount of uncertainty and threat in the environment."

In other words, when we believe we can take advantage of a situation, we literally become more powerful hunters. Our senses are heightened. We become excited. We embrace risk. But when we believe we're not masters of our universe, we dare less because we lose our nerve. So our challenge is to sustain our "swagger" independent of circumstance. We need to strike hard when we can but not doubt ourselves when we cannot.

So make every day a wolf day morning not a dog day afternoon.

BE RESILIENT - THE STARS ALIGN FOR THOSE WHO FIGHT THE GOOD FIGHT AND STAY THE COURSE

Resilience is the elasticity of champions. It enables them to spring back to their original strength and power after being blocked, beaten or battered. As the great boxing champion Jack Dempsey said, "the canvas is no place for a champion."

Life is a long game. Outside of a warzone, the human life expectancy is between 80 and 85 years. Champions make every season count. You can't win them all, but you can try. There's a direct correlation between ambition and longevity. If you keep on striving, you keep on growing. And if you keep on growing, time is your ally.

Dr. Tim Noakes is a professor of exercise and sports science at the University of Cape Town, South Africa. He has completed more than 70 marathons and ultra-marathons and is the author of Waterlogged, Running Injuries, Challenging Beliefs and the Lore of Running. Noakes has a fascinating insight into the linkage between mental and physical conditioning. He says, "With every stride the brain has to answer four questions, 'Are you going to stop, go the same speed, speed up or slow down?'"

"In the end," he says "I think all physical training comes down to mental training. The interesting thing about biology is if you train the same way every day, after about two months you are fully adapted – you don't make any new adaptations. The only thing you can change is your perception of what you can do. So the reason why you do long runs during marathon training is to convince your brain you can do it. I think that all training has an emotional component that is terribly, terribly important!

The very best athletes presume they're going to win and that's what they're focusing on all the time. Two Kenyans I spoke to recently said they see the mental effort as being greater than the physical effort in a marathon. The mental concentration – and not letting go at any moment – that's what's critical."

How long are your telomeres?

Here's the truth: some people are naturally more resilient than others. I'm not just talking about people who are fitter or healthier – although this obviously makes a big difference. I'm talking at a chromosomal level. At the end of every chromosome in our bodies, there is something called a "telomere." Telomeres are an essential part of human cells that affect how our cells age. Telomeres are the caps at the end of each strand of DNA. They protect our chromosomes, like the plastic tips at the end of shoelaces. Some of us have longer and stronger telomeres than others. They age slower. They withstand wear and tear better. If you have great telomeres, congratulations! You've won the genetic lottery. The rest of us have to earn our resilience through our thoughts and actions every day.

As someone who has wrestled with depression throughout my life, I know I'm not gifted with fantastic telomeres. My default position is not resilience. I feel the pain. I experience the loss. I lose my cool. I have to work very hard not to go soft. I understand the importance of mental and physical conditioning to sustain my performance, especially when things are not copacetic.

I'll confess, despite all my training, I'm still inclined to give up before I should. I'm still tempted to take the easy way out. I'm still intimidated by difficult people or tasks. But I'm also aware of the consequences of giving up. I'm cognizant of the self-disgust and futility that always accompanies wimping out. So I will do whatever it takes to avoid the false relief that presages intense remorse and regret.

I've also discovered it's never as scary or daunting as I think it might be. Every time I stay the course, I make another deposit on my resilience. I'm building my mental telomeres with every victory over my personal fragility. As Leonard Cohen sings, "There is a crack in everything. That's how the light gets in."

Resilience is a state of mind and body. The great football coach Vince Lombardi said, "Fatigue makes cowards of us all." When we're physically tired, we're mentally weak. Physical fitness enhances mental toughness. Stamina and resilience are joined at the hip. So design your daily physical workout schedule. Fine tune your physical machine so it becomes your most valuable resource. Don't sacrifice your health on the altar of busy-ness. Remember, if you don't find time to be healthy now, you will find time to get sick later.

What you eat shapes your mental health.

Just as you wouldn't put low-grade fuel into a high-performance machine, don't put junk food into yours.

Leslie Beck, a registered dietitian based at the Medisys clinic in Toronto, says the current evidence strongly links nutrition to mental health. Diet could be as important to psychiatry as it is to cardiology, endocrinology and gastroenterology. A high intake of fruits, vegetables, fish and whole grains can help protect you against depression.

On the other hand, it's not surprising a "junk food" diet can lead to a "junk mood" mindset. Hey, we're all exposed to an abundance of information on the power of healthy eating. But we often choose to ignore it because the temptation of junk food is just too strong to resist. I sometimes find myself mindlessly eating the wrong food, especially when I tell myself, "just this once." I always feel horrible afterwards.

There is always a healthy alternative. The secret is to be mindful in the moment. Nothing tastes as good as thinness feels. And nothing feels as good as a temptation resisted. So next time you're faced with food that tastes so good it's killing you, remember how good you'll feel after you resist it. Just as you would never reach for a cigarette in an airport or an airplane, don't reach for the double-bacon-cheeseburger anywhere.

Do you know your VO^2 max?

VO^2 max is the maximum amount of oxygen used during incremental exercise. It's regarded as the single best measure of cardiovascular fitness and aerobic power. If you have a high VO^2 max, your physical machine is running on high-octane gas. It's likely to outperform other machines running on lesser grade fuels. If all you do as a result of this book is consult your physician to measure your VO^2 max and find ways to enhance it, everything that I've written will be worthwhile.

Resilience is a team sport: relationships are your ultimate insurance against the trouble that's on the way.

All the social research indicates that building strong relationships builds resilience. The more people on your team, the greater your psychological wellbeing. You can only face the future because of the people who've got your back. Investing in your relationships is the best insurance you can have for the adversity and crises that are part of everyone's future.

Reach out and help someone today. Celebrate your relationships now. Acknowledge how important others are to you. Always be communicating. Seize every opportunity to declare your affection and gratitude. I never hear anyone say, "stop with all this appreciation." I constantly hear people lament the absence of the kudos they crave.

The quality of your closest relationships impacts your heart in the most literal way. Kira Birditt, a scientist at the Institute for Social Research at the University of Michigan, was the lead author of a study on how spousal relationships affected stress and blood pressure. She was quoted in The Globe and Mail (May 28, 2015) as saying, "We found that husbands had higher blood pressure when wives reported greater stress and that this link was even greater when husbands felt more negative about the relationship. In addition, when both members of the couple reported higher negative marital quality, they both had higher blood pressure." Yup, "happy wife happy life" is not just an idiom. It's a fact.

Neuroscientist David Eagleman (Financial Times, October 24, 2015) writes, "What does your brain need to function normally? Beyond the nutrients from the food you eat, beyond the oxygen you breathe, beyond the water you drink, there's something else, something equally as important: it needs other people. Normal brain function depends on the social web around us. Our neurons require other people's neurons to thrive and survive."

Every brain is a network of networks. We're only as good as the company we keep. And we only keep the company that we constantly earn. You have to be good company to keep good company.

Ultimately, resilience is a story that you tell yourself.

I joke in my seminars that I attend all my own seminars but it's true. Just like you, I make up stories about everything. I interpret my environment in ways that are habitual to me. Sometimes my stories are directly aligned with others' interpretation of events and sometimes I live in my own reality.

I've discovered champions tell themselves stories that empower them to carry on. Their stories express optimism, belief, caring, certainty and joy in happy endings. They focus on what they want, not what they wont. They are a yes-in-motion not a no-waiting-to-happen. So what's your story? Why would I want to hear it? How would I feel after listening to you? How do you feel after telling it?

Remember, a complainer never wins and a winner never complains. Listen to the vast majority of conversations around you and you'll hear people lamenting or lambasting the people around them. You'll hear the language of loss, anger, frustration or resentment. Champions, on the other hand, are acutely committed to telling stories celebrating their world or exploring ways to make it better. Every story in this book is designed to help you tell those kinds of stories.

BE A CATALYST THROUGH COLLABORATION – MULTIPLY OTHERS' POWER SO THEY CAN MAGNIFY YOURS

At a cellular level, everything is in ebb and flow. The big cycle of life is being awake and asleep. It's the generation of energy and the regeneration of energy. If you don't snooze, you will lose. There are moments we need to move and moments we need to be still. One empowers the other. Stillness without action is stagnation. But action without stillness is burnout.

We need to embrace our opposites. Our strengths always have a corresponding weakness. Our greatest moments are born in our lowest moments. There's a time to run hot: sexy, desirable, brilliant, amusing, fashionable, funny, extrovert and glowing. And a time to just be cool: serious, steady, reasonable, reliable, even-keeled, deliberate, traditional, solid.

Wherever we gain power, we lose it somewhere else. We need to be at peace with that. So I brand myself as: inspirational, energetic, ambitious, kinetic, charismatic, executional, intense, focused and goal oriented. I'm less gentle, cerebral, nurturing, analytic, peaceful, soft-spoken or balanced. I need to find the people who are strong where I am weak.

With differentiation comes deficit. When you pursue preeminence, you have to be willing to pay the price. Multiplying your strengths can deliver an exponential return, but trying to correct your weaknesses will be moderately successful at best and self-defeating at worse. So live with your weaknesses but balance them with someone else's strengths. That's the power of collaboration.

Think about how much effort it takes to correct your weakness. Think about how you even feel about doing it. It's a grudge activity at the best of times. It's never going to yield great results. Here's Lipkin's rule: work on your weakness so it won't be lethal to your success. Improve just enough to prevent it from tripping you up. Then find a wingman or wingwoman to complete you.

Creating a collaboration that complements our weaknesses requires huge self-awareness. It also demands we become attractive to others. If we don't know that we don't know, we don't know what to do or who to do it with. We also can't help anyone else or partner with anyone else. You're collaborating with me right now because I enticed you into reading this far. I've demonstrated how beneficial my strengths can be for you. Now you need to discover how you can package your strengths to others. They must want to partner with you. Just as you see what they can do for you, they must see what you can do for them.

You can be loud or you can be soft. You can be glossy or you can be grey. You can be out-there or you can be laid-back. But what must be immediately apparent is your benefit to others. Project your promise with authentic power. Remember: we are attracted to people who represent what we think we want. So ensure you're representing what you offer in a way that the right kind of people want it.

As a champion, your mission is to help others become a champion. Your energy and enthusiasm must make them energized and enthusiastic. Your presence must increase their self-awareness and multiply their capacity to be remarkable. If you become the conduit to their success, their success will flow back to you in rivers of abundance.

Doug Towill, a senior vice president at CI Investments, a leading Canadian investment company, defines the most valuable financial advisors as "transition Sherpas." I love it. A Sherpa is someone so skilled at carrying weight for others, he can help them surmount any obstacle. A Sherpa also enables others to shed their baggage so they can travel light. He understands it's his occupation, tradition and his calling to carry others' burdens for them. He doesn't complain, he just carries others to the top and then takes them back down again.

A catalyst is always civil. You can't bring people together by breaking them apart. There is a direct correlation between being nice and being wanted. Nice people are approachable. They make others feel respected because they are respectful. They lift them up by not putting them down.

Civil doesn't mean tame. It simply means adhering to the norms of politeness and courtesy that invite others to engage openly without fear of ridicule. Incivility shuts people down. There's no excuse for being rude. The inability to control your emotions can be extremely expensive in terms of lost opportunities and damaged relationships.

ACT YOUR ROLE

"All the world's a stage, And all the men and women merely players; They have their exits and their entrances, And one man in his time plays many parts." William Shakespeare, As You Like It

We love to watch great actors play great roles. While they're on stage or on screen, they become the people they're playing. We see the same actors playing multiple roles and we love them because they're so compelling. Leonardo DiCaprio can play Jay Gatsby or Jordan Belfort, The Wolf of Wall Street, with equal power. Jennifer Lawrence can morph from Katniss Everdeen, the super heroine in the Hunger Games, to Tiffany Maxwell, the depressed young widow in The Silver Linings Playbook. Denzel Washington can shape shift into any role he wants.

DiCaprio, Lawrence and Washington are professional actors – and so are you. Every day you get paid to play a role in other people's lives. You work in a company or with company. Your success is directly related to the confidence you instill in others, irrespective of how you feel. Sometimes, you can just "be yourself," and sometimes you need to work very hard at being who you need to be.

It's not about "faking it until you make it." That's a recipe for distrust and failure. It is about being an authentic actor. It's about understanding your personal value proposition and expressing it in the most impactful way. So my personal value proposition is to excite people into powerful action through unique insights. I have to perform my message, not just write it. I have to radiate passion and joie de vivre. I have to be animated and kinetic. I have to smile from the inside out. I have to be the best expression of motivator and coach that I can be. Sometimes it's easy. And sometimes I have to manufacture my authenticity. But here's the big *ah-ha*: the impact on my clients is the same. They get the value and the inspiration they expect and deserve. The impact on me is even greater: I build my motivational muscle. I go from blue to brilliant on demand. When you burn your excuses, the only option is success.

I study the great motivators, interviewers, champions, leaders and coaches. I also study great actors playing great motivators, interviewers, champions, leaders and coaches. Some of my primary sources of inspiration include: John Wooden, Jim Rohn, T.D. Jakes, David Letterman, Jimmy Fallon, Jerry Seinfeld, Charlie Rose, Winston Churchill, Nelson Mandela, Angela Ahrendts, Al Pacino in Any Given Sunday and Scent of a Woman, Denzel Washington in Remember the Titans, Gene Hackman in Hoosiers, Kurt Russell in Miracle on Ice, Daniel Day Lewis in The Last of the Mohicans and Meryl Streep in The Iron Lady to name a few.

The key point is see yourself playing the best version of your with every person every day. Separate you, the person, from you, the character. You're the person that only you can see. But you're also the character only other people can see. They infer who you are as a person by how they perceive your character. To the outside world, your character is the only thing that matters.

It's no coincidence that "character" has a double meaning. It's both the mental and moral qualities distinctive to an individual and a fictitious person in a novel, play or movie. When you act your role, you're dramatizing your mental and moral qualities to others so they can see who you truly are. Acting your role means rising above any situation to showcase your character.

It also lightens your performance anxiety. By acting your role, you are stepping into your superhero shoes. It's not you who is confronting the demons or taking on the bad guys, it's your alter ego or inner Superman. And as everyone knows, Superman always wins in the end.

When you act your role, you're always auditioning for the part. You have to know everything about it – the background, the hero, the relationship with other parts, the environment, the message and the expectations of the audience. When you win the part, you celebrate. When you lose the part, you mourn for a moment and then you move on.

One of the best things you can do it take an acting course. Begin with Dustin Hoffman's Masterclass on acting at masterclass.com

According to The New York Times (April 10, 2016), Peter Dinklage, who plays the role of Tyrion Lannister in the global smash hit Game of Thrones, shares the power of seeing yourself play the role even before you play the role: "Sometimes I work with some actors who aren't fully there. The guys in the visual effects department show you pre-visualizations. It used to be storyboards, but now they're really well done on computers and you see the whole scene with you and the animated dragons before you do it, so you get that in your head. It's neat. It's cool. I like it."

Imagine if you could see yourself playing your role perfectly before you play it so that you can play your role perfectly? Well you can imagine it. Scope it all out in your mind. Then follow your own pre-visualizations. In the end, everything is created twice – first in your mind, then in reality.

Every great actor has an agent that promotes her and finds her roles. You and I need to find our own agents. These are people so delighted with your contribution to their success they promote you passionately to others. You need to be one of these people. For example, I promote Mike Lipkin passionately not because I'm arrogant or self-centered, but because I believe in the Mike Lipkin character and his ability to excite audiences into powerful action.

REGENERATE YOURSELF

Whatever your generation, join the regeneration. Every sunrise is an invitation to recreate yourself in some shape, manner or form. Every time you do something or experience something new, you animate your life force.

Today, I've written 1500 words. I've conjured up thoughts from my mental depths I didn't know were there. Now I am inspired to conjure up thousands more. I love writing. I love speaking. I love sharing. I can only engage in these activities by finding new ways to engage in them.

Last week, I travelled to Mexico City for the first time. I delivered a program to a Latin American audience in the hospitality and travel industry. I was captivated by their generosity and passion. I learned about how to live in a city that is equal parts first and third worlds.

Yesterday I facilitated a conversation with a panel of experts in the new field of immuno-oncology, a whole new way to treat cancer patients versus conventional chemotherapy. I was stunned by the science, courage and compassion of health-care providers in this area. I left the session with an acute appreciation of the people who stand ready to help us fight our most dreaded diseases.

This morning, I read 60 pages of A Doubters Almanac by Ethan Canin. Canin is a hypnotic writer who casts his spell with every sentence. I can't wait to go back to his milieu.

Later this afternoon, I 'm meeting with colleagues to develop a script for a movie about building great business partnerships in the power and water industry. It's a brand new direction with brand new people.

Every day I commit to doing things that I've never done before. They're still within the realm of communication and inspiration, but they each have dimensions that impel me to learn new skills or insights. In my world, every day is a new career. And that's the way I like it. That's my vaccination against complacency.

George Bernard Shaw said youth is wasted on the young. I say youth is valued by the mature. The Websters Dictionary defines youth as "the time of life when someone is young." By that definition, youth is a state we never have to leave. It's a state that transcends age. But it's also a state that defies comfort. It demands extreme sports of a different nature. Instead of physically plunging down a slope on a snowboard or a mountain bike, we need to figuratively leap into the unknown. We need to find our own way of energizing ourselves into unprecedented action. What are you waiting for? This is the only moment you have. Tomorrow is not promised to anyone.

Hey, that's all I have to say.

I hope I've helped to regenerate your mojo. I hope something I've written jumpstarts your champion ambitions.

Let me know the impact that I've made on you. Feedback is the breakfast of champions. Write me at **mike.lipkin@environics.ca.**

This is Mike Lipkin and, until the next time, remember: It's all up to you now. Carry the torch. Travel light. Take others along for the ride.

MIKE LIPKIN

Mike Lipkin is president of Environics/Lipkin, a global research and motivation company based in Toronto. He is also an international strategic coach, facilitator and catalyst for high performance.

Mike combines his learning from talking to a million people in 43 countries with Environics Social Values research to offer clients the best of all worlds: a powerful blend of ideas and principles that help them achieve remarkable results.

Mike was raised in South Africa and emigrated to Canada in 2001. He is renowned for his ability to blend humour with content that inspires people into action.

Contact Mike to discover how he can help you and your team achieve champion results.

33 Bloor Street East, Suite 1020
Toronto, ON Canada
M4W 3H1
416.969.2822

www.mikelipkin.com